*Living for God's
pleasure*

Living for God's pleasure

The fruit of the Spirit

Derek Prime

EVANGELICAL PRESS

EVANGELICAL PRESS
Faverdale North Industrial Estate, Darlington, DL3 0PH,
England

Evangelical Press USA
P. O. Box 825, Webster, New York 14580, USA

e-mail: sales@evangelicalpress.org
web: http://www.evangelicalpress.org

First published 2004

British Library Cataloguing in Publication Data available

ISBN 0 85234 558 5

Printed and bound in Great Britain by Creative Print and Design
Wales, Ebbw Vale, South Wales.

Contents

1.

Prologue

'And now for listeners' questions.'

A panel of gardening and horticultural experts waits to answer questions from a studio audience for the benefit of radio listeners. 'First question, please?' invites the chairman. The questioner comes forward. 'I've wanted to produce grapes,' he explains. 'I planted my vines in a carefully chosen fertile place. I first dug up the ground and cleared it of stones. The vines were the very best. I made every provision for a good crop. I looked forward with delight to seeing them grow and tasting their fruit. But look at the samples I've brought with me! The vines have yielded only bad fruit.' Bitter disappointment shows itself in the owner's voice. What more could he have done?

The prophet Isaiah tells a similar story as a parable. The vineyard represented the Jewish people, and, as God's people, they were 'the garden of his delight' (Isaiah 5:7), a description that gives insight to how much his people mean to him. He anticipated the delight of seeing them grow in those virtues that would identify them as his people. The kind of fruit he looked for was justice and righteousness but, instead, he found violence and distress (Isaiah 5:1-7).

The picture of a vine and its fruit is used so frequently in the Old Testament that it was natural for Jews acquainted with their Scriptures to associate it with spiritual fruitfulness. It was as a vine that God brought them out of Egypt, drove out the opposing nations in Canaan, planted his people there and watched over them (Psalm 80:8, 14). The Lord Jesus Christ used the same picture to describe God's people (Luke 13:6-9).

The significance of the fruit of the Spirit in Galatians

The picture of fruit is found often in the Bible. For example, children are 'the fruit of the womb' (Deuteronomy 7:13) and those who refuse to listen to God will be 'filled with the fruit of their schemes' (Proverbs 1:31). In an environment where the fruits of the grape, pomegranate, fig, olive and apple were enjoyed, it is not surprising that the Christian virtues the Holy Spirit produces in the lives of believers should be described as 'fruit'. The phrase 'the fruit of the Spirit' appears uniquely in Galatians 5:22, although there are parallel expressions in the New Testament (e.g. Ephesians 5:9 and Philippians 1:11).

Paul's concern for the Galatians was that they might bear the kind of spiritual fruit that brings praise and pleasure to God. He expressed similar concern in other letters such as in Colossians 3:5-17, which has parallels with Galatians 5. An essential truth of the gospel is that salvation is the unique gift of God's grace in the Lord Jesus. It is not dependent for a moment upon any good works we may do, or upon a religious ritual or ceremony, such as circumcision or baptism. Sadly, the believers in Galatia were succumbing to the false teaching that circumcision was necessary for salvation. Paul wrote therefore with a sense of urgency.

The Galatian believers were not alone in this peril. Circumcision became a matter of controversy in the first-century church because some of the early Christians, who were Jews, required Gentile believers to be circumcised if they were to be received into the church (Acts 15:1). The Council at Jerusalem resolved the issue by determining that it should not be obligatory for Gentiles (vv. 1-21). However, those of 'the circumcision group' or Judaizers still hankered after such a requirement (Galatians 2:12; Titus 1:10).

Paul and other Christian leaders recognized the danger of the Judaizers' influence. If believers followed their teaching they would soon abandon their total dependence upon the saving work of the Lord Jesus Christ for salvation and instead rely upon law-keeping and the outward sign of circumcision. To follow such teaching was to abandon the freedom Christians rightly enjoy through the Lord Jesus Christ and, instead, to burden themselves with a form of slavery (Galatians 5:1). Paul was astonished that they were so quickly deserting the one who had called them by the grace of Christ and were turning to a different gospel that was no gospel at all (1:6-7).

In Christ neither circumcision nor uncircumcision has any value. The only thing that matters is a right relationship with God through new birth and its fruits (Galatians 5:6; 6:15; cf. 1 Corinthians 7:19; Colossians 2:11), and not least in the fruit of the Spirit. The only thing that counts is faith; that is, faith in the Lord Jesus Christ — expressing itself through love (Galatians 5:6) and, we might add, all that goes with love, as seen in the fruit of the Spirit. The fruit of the Spirit is a consequence of our Lord Jesus Christ rescuing us from this present evil world, according to the will of our God and Father, and the glory is rightly his (1:4-5). Its growth in us is a proof of the authenticity of the gospel we have received and believed (vv. 6-12). It is a direct consequence of the Lord Jesus Christ living in us (2:20) through our reception of his gift of the Holy Spirit (3:2, 14), so that we have become sons and daughters of God (3:26-27; 4:6-7).

The 'badge' of Christian discipleship is not circumcision but love (John 13:35). The Judaizers emphasized outward externals rather than spiritual life and its fruit. Paul had come to understand that for a Jew circumcision only had value if it expressed the 'circumcision of the heart, by the Spirit', so that a man lived for God's pleasure (Romans 2:28-29). Spiritual life is living by the Spirit, that is to say, depending upon him and deliberately obeying him as he points us to the Lord Jesus and encourages us to model our lives on his.

The aptness of the picture

The picture of fruit was particularly apt in the first century since most people came from an agricultural background, and it remains appropriate.

Fruitfulness is what God requires from the beginning of our Christian life. As soon as he calls us to faith in his Son, he calls us to repentance and *the fruit* it produces. While repentance is not once for all, since the Christian life calls for daily repentance and turning from sin, it is one of the initial fruits of new birth and conversion.

As John the Baptist prepared the way for the Lord Jesus Christ, he focused people's minds on producing *fruit* in keeping with repentance (Matthew 3:8; Luke 3:8). Expected fruit included generous sharing, justice and fairness, thoughtfulness and contentment (Luke 3:10-14).

Proof of life

The picture of fruit is also apt because it is always the consequence and proof of life. The new life we possess as Christian believers flows from our union with the Lord Jesus Christ in his death, resurrection and ascension. Our spiritual union with him makes utterly reasonable our expectation of his Spirit's fruit.

The Lord Jesus explained that true disciples are recognizable by their fruit (Matthew 7:20; Luke 6:43-45). The fruit of the Spirit is the natural lifestyle of those in whom the Spirit lives and who follow his direction. It is not produced by commandment or law but by life. If we want to know if a fruit tree is alive and healthy, the evidence is its fruit. If we want to know whether we are spiritually alive and healthy, the verification is the fruit of God's Spirit in us. The New Testament constantly warns of the danger of self-deception and spiritual complacency. We are encouraged to examine and test ourselves to see whether we are in the faith. If Jesus Christ lives in us by his Spirit then there will be fruit to prove it, and there are no exceptions (2 Corinthians 13:5-6).

Importance of spiritual feeding

The picture of fruit is further apt because it points to the importance of spiritual feeding. In the story with which we began, the planter of the vines put them in a fertile environment. Essential to the health of a fruit-producing vine is that the soil in which it is planted provides necessary nutrients for growth.

Basic to the provision God makes for our spiritual growth is his word, the Scriptures of the Old and New Testaments. In the parable of the sower, it is those who accept the word who bear fruit (Mark 4:20). The Bible is in our hands to read, and the Lord Jesus Christ provides teachers and preachers to communicate it to us in digestible meals.

Using the picture of a fruitful tree, the writer of the first psalm — a psalm that sets the pattern for the whole book of Psalms — describes an individual who is in a right relationship with God in these terms:

He is like a tree planted by streams of water,
    which yields its fruit in season
and whose leaf does not wither.
    Whatever he does prospers

(Psalm 1:3).

At whatever stage we are in the Christian life, adequate and
correct feeding is fundamental. It is no accident that the longest
psalm, Psalm 119, illustrates more than any other part of the
Bible the power of God's Word to direct and nourish our spiritual growth.

A number of years ago the great vine at Hampton Court, a
palace on the River Thames in London, especially associated
with Henry VIII, began to give signs that its ability to bear fruit
was on the wane. Careful investigations were made, and down
among the roots of the vine were found the remains of ancient
foundations that were secretly obstructing its legitimate growth.
The embedded obstacles were excavated, and the cavity was
filled with fifty to sixty tons of earth. It was not long before the
liberated tree revealed unprecedented fertility. As we travel on
our Christian journey, God indicates hindrances to our spiritual
growth, often remainders of our old life still imbedded in our
mind-set and lifestyle, obstacles that hinder our effective feeding upon his Word and our fellowship with him. As we face up
to them — excavate and remove them — renewed growth,
spiritual vitality and fruitfulness follow.

At no stage in life should we neglect to check for 'remainders
of our old life' that threaten our spiritual fruitfulness. Basic to
Christian experience is the constant battle between the desires
of our sinful nature and what the Spirit wants for us (Galatians
5:17). When I was first converted, I imagined that when I became older and more mature — like those who were examples
to me of godliness — the battle would be less or even non-
existent! But the truth is that the battle is unceasing. Every day

I need to die to what I know belongs to my old life and instead 'keep in step with the Spirit' (5:25) by offering myself afresh to God (Romans 6:13). That is the necessary path to fruitfulness.

Careful pruning

The picture of fruit is especially appropriate since the successful production of the best fruit in the world of nature usually requires careful pruning, or in spiritual language, discipline and chastisement. This is underlined by the Lord Jesus: 'I am the true vine, and my Father is the gardener. He cuts off every branch in me that bears no fruit, while every branch that does bear fruit he *prunes* so that it will be even more fruitful' (John 15:1-2).

We are not to think of chastisement and discipline invariably as punishment for sin and misdemeanours, but rather as God's method of ensuring that we are bearing fruit. Paul discovered that if he was going to be fruitful in character and service, there was a sense in which he had to 'die every day' (1 Corinthians 15:31). He was pruned by experiences of personal weakness (2 Corinthians 12:7-10), loneliness (2 Timothy 4:16-18) and troubles (2 Corinthians 1:4).

At every stage in the Christian life, difficult experiences are like careful snips of a gardener's pruning knife. Faith's development of fruit often requires trials, such as chastisement, disappointments, illness and suffering. Yet, in permitting them, God always has our increased fruitfulness in view. As we are trusting and submissive to him, they are ploughed into our lives as necessary nutrients or fertilizers to produce a harvest of righteousness and peace (Hebrews 12:11), for God's honour and the good of others. Consequently, we are able to 'rejoice in our sufferings, because we know that suffering produces perseverance; perseverance, character; and character, hope. And hope does not disappoint us, because God has poured out his love

into our hearts by the Holy Spirit, whom he has given us'
(Romans 5:3-5).

Charles Simeon was a minister in Cambridge in the late eighteenth and early nineteenth centuries (1759-1836). His ministry
received a mixed reception as he faithfully taught God's Word.
His biographer records: 'By learning to accept his unpopularity
Simeon became gradually less aggressive. He says he found
great comfort and assurance in the passage of Scripture which
runs: "The servant of the Lord must not strive", and he used to
repeat it to himself "hundreds of times". In a letter to a very
close friend, Thomas Lloyd, he showed something of what the
months of strain and humiliation were teaching him: "They who
are most earnest in prayer for grace, are often most afflicted,
because the graces which they pray for, e.g. faith, hope, patience, humility, etc. are only to be wrought in us by means of
those trials which call forth the several graces into act and
exercise."'[1]

A profound paradox of the Christian life is that the way to
fruitfulness is death. Not referring to character forming, but to
the cross, our Lord Jesus said, 'I tell you the truth, unless a
grain of wheat falls to the ground and dies, it remains only a
single seed. But if it dies, it produces many seeds' (John 12:24).
That principle of death as a condition of a rich harvest is written into the Christian life, not in small print, but large. Pruning
is something in which we ourselves are to engage. Our putting
to death 'the acts of the sinful nature' is a necessary consequence of our union with the Lord Jesus in his crucifixion, and
the fruit of the Spirit is part of our sharing in his risen life.

The immediate context of this passage in Galatians in which
Paul describes the fruit of the Spirit is the description of the acts
of the sinful nature or *the bad fruit of our old life*: 'sexual immor-
ality, impurity and debauchery; idolatry and witchcraft; hatred,
discord, jealousy, fits of rage, selfish ambition, dissensions,
factions and envy; drunkenness, orgies, and the like' (5:19-21).

The fruit of the Spirit — the fruit of our new self — appears and flourishes as we prune, or put to death, these sad aspects of our old life. Essential to our new life, as those who belong to the Lord Jesus, is the crucifying of the sinful nature with its passions and desires (5:24) so that we make room for the Spirit's fruit to grow.

2.

Love

It is no accident that love comes first in the description of the fruit of the Spirit. All other aspects of the fruit flow from it, and convey it. Think for a moment of the different appliances in use in our homes. Perhaps our morning begins with the ringing of a clock radio alarm. We then enjoy a cup of tea or coffee by means of an electric kettle that boils the water. We turn on our radio to hear the morning's news. They all depend on the same source — the electricity flowing from our local power station.

The dynamic of Christian character and life

Augustine was right when he said, 'Love God and do what you like.' When love is in place, everything else slots into position. Where love is found, the other aspects of the Spirit's fruit grow in its fertile soil.

While everyone knows what love is — or, sadly, sometimes, what it is like to live without it — it is the most difficult feature of the Spirit's fruit to define. The different Greek words used for love illustrate this, as does our contemporary use of the word.

The first of these words is *eros*, which expresses the love of a man for a woman, and vice versa. Our word 'erotic' is derived from it, with its sexual implications, many of them unhelpful. It refers to a love that has passion, intoxication and ecstasy. Uncontrolled, it becomes lust. For those who have not experienced true love, love tends to be thought of mainly in sexual terms. George Orwell's writings provide a sad example of erotic sexual love. Describing what he calls 'the supreme moment of love', he wrote, 'It is nothing, an instant, a second perhaps. A second of ecstasy, and after that — dust and ashes, nothingness.' He goes on to write, 'I was left cold and languid, full of vain regrets.'[1] *Eros* is not used at all in the New Testament, not because God regards it as unimportant, especially in relation to marriage, but because it is not the kind of love we are urged to cultivate.

Then comes *philia*, which is the warm love we feel for those close and dear to us. It has to do with the feelings of our heart. The Bible usually employs this Greek word when it refers to brotherly love, although it may sometimes use *agape*. Christian fellowship is an expression of this love as we appreciate our family relationship in Christ. Galatians 6:1-3 illustrates the practice of brotherly love. It is all too easy to pass harsh judgement on those who are overcome by sin. Love does not pretend sin does not exist but acts to restore the person overtaken by it.

Storgē equals affection, and is used especially of the love of parents and children. Undeniably, they know a unique love for each other. While it may vary in degree from family to family, we expect it to exist as it is a common element of human experience.

The distinctively Christian word *agape*, however, is what is used here in the fruit of the Spirit, and it is this that we must explore. Rather than providing a definition immediately, we will attempt to do so at the end.

The proper starting point

The place to begin is the character of God, since the fruit of the Spirit is essentially his character produced and reflected in his spiritual children, for that is what we are as God's people. The Bible, and especially the New Testament, affirms that God is love (e.g. 1 John 4:8, 16). This does not mean that God is only love, but it points to love as one of his major characteristics, along with the important attribute or quality of holiness. The apostle John declares, therefore, that God is both love and light (1 John 1:5; 4:16).

All 'agape' love comes from God. His love for his creatures is such that 'He causes his sun to rise on the evil and the good, and sends rain on the righteous and the unrighteous' (Matthew 5:45). Wherever 'agape' love is found, God is its source since it is the reflection of the Creator in the creature. Every aspect of God's relationship to his people is marked by his love.

The demonstration of God's love

The New Testament always takes us to the same event — the cross of our Lord Jesus Christ — as the greatest demonstration and proof of God's love. God has shown his love through a single act of eternal significance in human history. He sent his one and only Son into the world with the specific purpose of becoming the atoning sacrifice for our sins.

In the work of the cross

The death of Christ is hub of the Bible. While there are truths we learn and from which we move on to others, we never move on from this amazing and fundamental explanation of our salvation. There is always more to understand, and greater depths to plumb. Christians throughout the ages have not chosen a manger, an empty tomb or a throne to symbolize Christianity, but the cross. To look at it, and to recognize our dependence upon the saving work of our Lord Jesus Christ, is like pressing the automatic focus button on a camera. With the cross as the focal point, all else finds its proper focus. As we fix our eyes upon Christ's death for us, we grow in our appreciation of God's love. But to appreciate this love, we must constantly explore and ponder it.

It is a love that has no regard to our merits since we are sinners who deserve God's anger and righteous condemnation. God's love is an exercise of his divine will in deliberate choice, made without assignable reason, except what lies in his nature (Deuteronomy 7:7-8). Our love, on the other hand, tends to be influenced by the attractiveness and attainments of its objects.

The world makes the most fuss of those who are outwardly attractive. Not so, however, with God's love. Brian Mawhinney, a former British government minister, recalls a wise and spiritual Christian telling him: 'Remember Brian, there is nothing you can ever do, or achieve, that will make God love you more; and there is nothing you can ever do, however bad, that will make God love you less. And the measure of God's love for you is already set. He gave His Son to die for you'.[2] Only as we understand how much God the Father loves his Son, Jesus Christ, can we begin to measure the cost of his sending his Son to suffer his necessary judgement upon our sin. Nowhere do we see God's love more than in his Son's death for us, and therefore nothing is more important in the Christian life than keeping our eyes upon that cross, and living in the light of it.

In the immeasurable nature of God's love

'Your love, O LORD, reaches to the heavens,' the writer of the psalm declares (36:5; 57:10). Not only so, it is 'higher than the heavens' (108:4). His love is a kind of yardstick or benchmark. We are encouraged to reason with ourselves: 'If God loves us like that, how can we doubt his willingness to give us through his Son all that we need in this life and the next?' 'If God loves us like that, how can we question his love when suffering or disappointments come to us?' 'If God loves us like that, how wonderful is the privilege of becoming his children!' God always loves us with the intensity of love seen at Calvary. This is a truth we should ponder regularly.

The image of the invisible God

As we consider the life and ministry of our Lord Jesus as revealed in the four Gospels, we see God's love in its perfection. While the Father *sent* his Son to be the Saviour (1 John 4:9), it was the Son's love for the Father and for us that caused him to come with the explicit purpose of dying for our sins in order to become the 'one mediator between God and men' (1 Timothy 2:5). The love shown then is the love he has for his people now. He 'loves us [note the *present* tense] and has freed us from our sins by his blood' (Revelation 1:5). The Lord Jesus drew attention to his death as the supreme demonstration of his love: 'Greater love has no one than this, that he lay down his life for his friends' (John 15:13). At the heart of Christian experience is the truth that 'The life I live in the body, I live by faith in the Son of God, who loved me and gave himself for me' (Galatians 2:20).

Two passages in the Gospels illustrate the practical and glorious nature of our Saviour's love. The first is the account of the illness and death of Lazarus in John 11. The two sisters, Martha and Mary, sent a message to Jesus: 'Lord, the one you *love* is sick' (John 11:3). John confirms the accuracy of this description of Lazarus when he writes, 'Jesus *loved* Martha and her sister and Lazarus' (11:5) and when he notes the comment of the crowd: 'See how he *loved* him!' (11:36). The record of Jesus' love for Lazarus and his two sisters assures us of his love for us likewise as individuals.

The second passage is John 13 where immediately before the Passover Feast, on the night Jesus was forsaken by the disciples, John records, 'Having loved his own who were in the world, he now showed them the full extent of his *love*' or, as it has it in the Authorized Version, 'He *loved* them to the end' (John 13:1). In spite of all their failures, he loved them still. They made the great discovery that his love was not at all dependent upon either their worthiness or achievements. Little wonder that Paul describes our Lord Jesus Christ's love as surpassing knowledge (Ephesians 3:19). No matter how much we find out about it, there are oceans more to discover. As F. M. Lehman wrote:

> Could we with ink the ocean fill,
> And were the skies of parchment made,
> Were every stalk on earth a quill,
> And every man a scribe by trade,
> To write the love of God above,
> Would drain the ocean dry.
> Nor could the scroll contain the whole,
> Though stretched from sky to sky.[3]

The love the Lord Jesus showed for his disciples was not a doting or foolishly indulgent love, but a love that always had their best interests in view. Essential to it were those occasions when he rebuked them for their failures, lack of insight and folly (Matthew 16:22; Mark 8:32-33; Matthew 19:13; Luke 9:55), but never in contradiction of his love. So it is with us today (Revelation 3:19).

Here we meet a great challenge: Jesus Christ's love for us is the required pattern and model of the love we are to have for others since Jesus said, 'A new command I give you: Love one another. As I have loved you, so you must love one another' (John 13:34). A remarkable consequence of new birth is that the love of Christ increasingly controls us so that we set no bounds to what the practice of love may cost us, to the point where the world may think we are crazy (2 Corinthians 5:13-14).

Satisfaction and security in God's love

The greatest characteristic of the most godly men and women throughout the centuries has been their appreciation of God's love and its reflection in their lives — the two are inseparable. When we become God's spiritual children, he pours his love into our hearts. While we might interpret this as meaning that he enables us to love others (which is true), we are meant to understand that primarily he shows us how much he loves us. Moreover — significantly, because we are thinking of the fruit of the Spirit — he does this by the Holy Spirit: 'God has poured out his love into our hearts by the Holy Spirit, whom he has given us' (Romans 5:5).

Revealed by the Spirit

The Spirit's unique prerogative is to reveal to our souls the love God has for us. Usually he does this by means of his own word, as we read it or hear it taught and preached. Then that love holds us delightfully captive. We find ourselves saying, whatever our circumstances, 'We *know* and *rely* on the love God has for us' (1 John 4:16).

Prompts growth in our love

Every fresh appreciation of God's love prompts growth in our expression of love — first to God himself, then to his spiritual children and to everyone. We love him because he first loved us (1 John 4:19). Significantly, the Lord Jesus spoke to early Christians of their '*first*-love' for him (Revelation 2:4). The initial experience of the forgiveness of our sins produces a great burst of love for God, that hopefully remains an ever-flowing river as we grasp more and more of that love's infinite dimensions.

The more we love God, the more we know him to be our best possession, the chief happiness and joy of our soul (Psalm

16:2). The more we appreciate the cross, the more we ask ourselves: 'If God has given me the Lord Jesus Christ, what more
can I ask or want?' We can add our agreement to Psalm 73:25:
'Whom have I in heaven but you? And earth has nothing I
desire besides you.'

No peace or rest compares with resting in God's love. But
there is a vital consequence. The most important way to show
to the world that we are God's children and disciples of his Son
is to display his love for others through our conduct. It is not
enough to say to people 'God loves you'. Our behaviour must
prove it.

Visible to our enemies

Early Christians so showed their love that their enemies spoke
of it. The Roman Emperor Julian (332-63) was furious that
many were drawn to the Christian faith because of what they
saw of Christian love in practice. Writing of the Christian faith,
he said that it 'has been specially advanced through the loving
service rendered to strangers, and through their care for the
burial of the dead. It is a scandal that there is not a single Jew
who is a beggar, and that the godless Galileans care not only
for their own poor but for ours as well; while those who belong
to us look in vain for the help that we should give them'.[4]

The priority of love

Not only is love the first aspect of the Spirit's fruit but it is also
the most important spiritual gift. Paul wrote about spiritual gifts
to the church at Corinth — a Christian community that over-
rated some of the most spectacular gifts. Fundamental to his
answer to their problem was the pinpointing of the priority of
love. 1 Corinthians 13 is the passage our contemporary world
often chooses to read on important occasions, especially at

weddings, but usually without recognizing the impossibility of its achievement without God's Spirit.

Love has priority over the gift of tongues, the gift of prophecy, the gifts of knowledge and teaching, the gift of exceptional faith, the special gift of the ability and willingness to give generously, and that of complete dedication to an ideal, even if it requires death for its sake. Paul could not have put it more plainly (vv. 1-3).

Love is to be the foremost aim of all Christians (1 Corinthians 14:1), and this cannot be said of any other of God's gifts or aspects of his Spirit's fruit. Love is the commandment the Lord Jesus established for his disciples as the chief characteristic of his kingdom: 'A new command I give you: Love one another. As I have loved you, so you must love one another' (John 13:34). He said this just after he had washed their feet! Love is the one continuing debt we owe to one another (Romans 13:8).

In his commentary on Galatians, Jerome (c. 345-419) tells the story of the apostle John in his old age when he lived in Ephesus. He used to be carried into the congregation in the arms of his disciples and was unable to say anything except 'Little children, love one another.' At last, wearied that he always spoke the same words, they asked, 'Master, why do you always say this?' 'Because,' he replied, 'it is the Lord's command, and if this only is done, it is enough.'[5]

Love's priority is all the greater when we recognize that the love we express to others is the love we show to Jesus Christ. There will be many delightful surprises on the Day of Judgement when he says to some, 'Whatever you did for one of the least of these brothers of mine, you did for me' (Matthew 25:40).

Love at work

1 Corinthians 13 describes love at work. Love is never inactive. It always does what it does not have to do and what might not be asked for or expected.

Patient

Love is patient with people (v. 4). We cannot live and work with others without aspects of their characters, and perhaps eccentricities, irritating us, as ours probably do them. Love is tolerant and works hard at being uncomplaining. It makes allowances for people, for practically anything.

Kind

Close on the heels of patience comes kindness (v. 4), especially expressed in gentleness. Love does not mean never being honest and truthful about difficulties in relationships, but rather endeavouring to do so without unnecessary offence. Augustine said, 'Love me and then say anything to me and about me you like.' Richard Baxter was a godly pastor in Kidderminster in the seventeenth century. His people said of him, 'We take all things well from one who always and wholly loves us.'[6] When Charles Simeon, the minister of Holy Trinity Church, Cambridge, died, the preacher at his funeral spoke of the 'love which ever beamed' on Simeon's face.[7] Kenneth MacRae, a minister in the Free Church of Scotland, began his ministry in Lochgilphead. Writing in his diary one Saturday night after a meeting, he wrote of a godly elder who 'looked love'.[8] When we 'look love', we deal with difficulties without offending.

Joyful

Perhaps surprisingly, joy comes next (v. 6), although this refers to a special kind of joy. It is a joy about the truth in contrast to delight in evil. Something in our fallen human nature finds pleasure in hearing bad and unpleasant things about others. Love genuinely rejoices in good news about people because it is not jealous of them and wants their highest good.

Protective

Love is protective of others (v. 7), and not least of their reputations and interests. Rather than doubting people, it trusts them, always hoping for the best for and from them. These are not occasional attitudes but a persevering frame of mind that never fails to operate (v. 8).

Love's opposites

The attractiveness of love is underlined in 1 Corinthians 13 by expressions of its opposites. While perhaps obvious, they are challenging to consider.

Envy

First comes envy (v. 4). If we allow ourselves to be jealous of people, we soon stop loving them.

Boastfulness and pride (v. 4)

When we boast we put ourselves before, and above, others. By what we say, we may make others feel inferior. Parents, for example, should not boast about their children — or even talk too much about them — especially to those who are not blessed with families. Love creates sensitivity to other people's viewpoint so that whatever we say and do is calculated to make them comfortable and at ease.

Rudeness, selfishness, irritability and touchiness (v. 5)

Rudeness usually arises from selfishness, and selfishness is neither more nor less than love of ourselves above others. If we are proud of our attainments or position, we may be tempted to be rude and touchy, but it does us no credit. It is sad if people have to watch carefully what they say to us in case we are offended, or perhaps because they do not say 'thank you' for something we have done.

Resentment and malice (v. 5)

Love harbours no resentment, and keeps no record of wrongs as the memory function of an electronic calculator keeps a record of a past calculation. Instead, it presses the cancel button so that there is no record of them. Love reflects God's love in showing kindness even to its enemies, endeavouring to emulate the consistent love the Lord Jesus shows us. We may need to be challenged about the reality of our love for our enemies.

Love in its working clothes

The more we love, the more we feel the need to love more. Never satisfied with our attainment of love, we want it to grow, increase and overflow. We learn not to be selective in the objects of our love, but rather to love everyone in the same way, demonstrating how different this *agape* love is from ordinary human love.

Extends to all

Love sees all other Christians as brothers and sisters and all who are not Christians as neighbours. This is not without effort — effort that God's Spirit inspires. This love is not so much a question of our feelings but a matter of will and action, a principle by which we live. It does not ask, 'Do I like or love this person?' but rather, 'How may I act in love towards him or her?'

A Christian in a university town was asked to befriend a young man leaving home for the first time and beginning at the university. He duly got in touch with him and invited him to his home. Immediately he recognized that the young man was not the kind of person he would naturally choose to be a friend. There was almost a natural antipathy. Realizing that this was not a proper Christian response, he chose to act towards him as he knew Christian love dictates. To his amazement, this young man became one of his best friends.

Requires effort

Throughout the centuries, Christians have recognized the effort and determination love requires. One of the first missionaries to join William Carey in India was John Mack, from Charlotte Chapel, Edinburgh. Letters were infrequent but those that survive show that relationships were a challenge to Christian character. Christopher Anderson, his pastor, wrote to him in March 1827, honestly addressing the challenge.

> In each of you there exist, it is true, the remains of sin, and each is clothed in a body of sin and death, and each may be different in regard to natural constitution; but, my dear brother, what does this signify? ... And what do you say to the fulness that is in Jesus? Draw upon it daily, hourly, for fervent love to each other, notwithstanding all your imperfections and shortcomings. Never mind, still resolve to love each other, and more and more. Pray for this. *But* for the love so beautifully delineated by God himself in the 13th of 1st Cor., any Church, any little circle of saints, would soon prove more hideous than the crater of Vesuvius. May the dew of divine love and mercy descend upon you, and make you a blessing to generations yet unborn.[9]

Love is not a matter of sentiment but something we deliberately set ourselves to achieve.

Must be sincere and genuine

Love aims at sincerity and genuineness since something of the hypocrite exists in us all. Actions can be governed by a desire to be thanked or thought spiritual, whereas the good of others is to be our proper motive. *Agape* love does not desire something for itself but wants to give, without ulterior purpose. Its object is to follow the pattern of the Lord Jesus' love even if it means personal sacrifice. As salt brings out the flavour in potatoes, so love adds flavour to Christian testimony in an often insipid and unloving world.

Serves others

Love always has its working clothes on in practical, down-to-earth and willing service of others and in generous sharing to meet their needs. It starts in the home, where everything needs to begin. Some children were asked, 'What is love?' The answer of one little girl was significant: 'Love is when the person reading you a bedtime story doesn't skip any of the pages.'

Love's qualities are essentially positive in that they always build up, unite and bind all other virtues together in perfect unity.

We are now in a position to attempt a definition of this love. **The love required of us is a totally unselfish love, an unconquerable benevolence, a matter of will and action, expressed in service of the undeserving as much as of the deserving, based upon the pattern of the love set forth in the cross of our Lord Jesus Christ.**

Love's unique permanence

Love is the permanent priority of the Christian life. Basic to all Christian ethics, it is to inform and dictate every action. It remains the principal test of our Christian profession. If we declare ourselves followers of Jesus Christ and members of God's family, all who know us are entitled to test what we say by our love (1 John 3:10, 14-15; 4:7-8, 12, 16).

When other spiritual gifts pass away, and are unnecessary, love will remain. Love is the atmosphere of heaven, and it is there that we shall know its full beauty and wonder. Meanwhile we are to know that whatever else may be a priority, love comes top of the list.

Spiritual growth and effective witness

It is only as we are rooted and established in love that we increase our personal capacity to take in the amazing dimensions of our Lord Jesus Christ's love and know God better (Ephesians 3:17-19). This makes eminently good sense since God is love. To know him is to appreciate more his love and to feel the privilege and obligation to express it in our lives.

This expression of love to others is essential to Christian witness in the world. Like men and women as a whole, many of our natures are hard, cold and selfish. None of us loves others as much as we ought. But as God's Spirit works in us, producing his fruit, he enables us to love one another as brothers and sisters, and to love those who are not yet members of God's family. This love has a unique winsomeness. While faith gives us the confidence that others can be won, love is faith's chosen instrument to accomplish it.

Practical action

It helps me to address the following exhortations to myself.

- Avoid glibness about love and loving one another. It requires more than just talk or singing about it.
- Acknowledge attitudes and actions that are contrary to love. Love demands that I should be truthful with myself. I need to identify the people I find it most difficult to love. Again, honesty is imperative.
- Covenant to pray for them, and to seek their well-being.
- Think about how I can deliberately act towards them by specific acts of love.
- Pray for the Spirit's help. He is there to implement the spiritual desires, ambitions and resolves he prompts within me.
- Every time I meet around the Lord's Table with other Christian believers, I should examine my love — both for my Saviour Jesus Christ and for others.

3.
Joy

Joy walks hand in hand with love. Experience teaches that where love exists, joy quickly follows upon its heels. What makes homes happy is not the possession of wealth, but the practice of love. Having used the word 'happy', however, we must be quick to distinguish between happiness and joy. Happiness tends to be associated with pleasant circumstances and is invariably linked with health, success and possessions. The uniqueness of joy is that it can be experienced even when we are ill, unsuccessful, and not well off financially. Surroundings and circumstances tend to determine happiness, whereas joy shapes our attitude to them.

The joy that is the Spirit's fruit is *not* the result of agreeable circumstances, but an inward joy springing up within us, like a living fountain, irrespective of what our circumstances or difficulties may be. It is like an oasis in a desert, an irrepressible consequence of the experience of salvation — one of God's gifts through his Son.

Christian joy

What makes Christian joy special is that God himself is its author and object. He loves joy and delights in cheerfulness.

The joy he gives is a joy of the heart or soul or spirit, that is to say, our innermost being. It has the capacity to displace worry at the centre of our life. Difficulties may even serve to make this joy more meaningful and remarkable. In the early days of the church Peter and John were punished and imprisoned because of their public preaching about Jesus. But on their release they were 'rejoicing because they had been counted worthy of suffering disgrace for the Name' (Acts 5:41). Many years later, writing to scattered Christians in Asia Minor, Peter urged, 'Dear friends, do not be surprised at the painful trial you are suffering, as though something strange were happening to you. But rejoice that you participate in the sufferings of Christ, so that you may be overjoyed when his glory is revealed' (1 Peter 4:12-13).

Joy in the Father and the Son

Christian joy is joy in God and in his Son, our Lord Jesus Christ. Its focus is on God's character and what he may always be relied upon to do. It finds its rest in his attributes, shouting 'Hallelujah' — whether with the voice or in the heart — at every new appreciation of his sovereignty, holiness, mercy and love. Fresh understanding of God's character prompts joy. Most of all, it rejoices in God's saving acts (Psalm 5:11; 9:2; 16:9). As Paul aptly expresses it: 'We ... rejoice in God through our Lord Jesus Christ, through whom we have now received reconciliation' (Romans 5:11). At its heart is the joy of salvation. What men and women of faith in the Old Testament eagerly anticipated for many centuries is our present possession (Isaiah 12:3).

While those who are not Christians may also know a joy distinct from happiness, Christian joy is unique because God the Holy Spirit conveys it to us, making it independent of people and possessions. The Spirit's power, being that of God, is almighty, and nothing can frustrate his communication of joy. It is a joy that already has something of the anticipation of heaven about it, putting it beyond our ability to express in words. It is more secure than any other joy because its source is not in human relationships but in our relationship with our unchanging God and Saviour. Since he is everlasting, so is the joy we know. In the life to come it will be immeasurably enhanced by the total absence of sin and sorrow.

Sure foundations

The test of joy, as it is of happiness, is how well it weathers the storms of life. Here Christian joy excels and outshines all competitors. Nothing life throws at us can touch its foundations. An essential part of it is the joy of having being found by our Heavenly Father — the joy of salvation, to which we have referred. The joy the prodigal son knew, as his father put his forgiving arms around him, is ours. The joy of salvation is the joy of forgiveness, reconciliation to God, justification through faith, acceptance with God and eternal union with our Lord Jesus Christ.

Fellowship with God

Vital to Christian joy is the joy of a new life. Our spiritual union with the Lord Jesus not only identifies us with him in his death but also means that we may live a new life by the power of his resurrection, imparted to us by his Spirit. We are given a fresh start, with new perspectives upon life and eternity. At the heart of the development and growth of this new life is the privilege of personal fellowship with God the Father, God the Son and God the Holy Spirit. Since this is what we were originally created for, it is no surprise that it is here we find our deepest and most satisfying joy.

Through the ministry of the Holy Spirit, God the Father and God the Son delight to come and make their home with us. The Lord Jesus may then choose to show himself to our souls, especially when we most need that unique benefit (John 14:21, 23), as he did to Stephen when he was prepared to lay down his life for his Master (Acts 7:55-56). Our joy has the Lord Jesus as its special object and is enhanced every time we turn our thoughts to him (Philippians 4:4). A sight of him is the best answer to all our troubles.

Samuel Rutherford (1600-1661) was imprisoned in Aberdeen because of his faithfulness to the gospel. He wrote letters from prison to his congregation and friends at Anwoth. In one of these letters he writes of the Lord Jesus, 'He is my song in the night... For the most part my life is joy, and such joy through His comforts ... I can scarce bear what I get: Christ giveth me a measure heaped up, pressed down, and running over...'[1]

Fellowship with other believers

From the joy of fellowship with God flows the matching joy of fellowship with other Christian believers, without regard to age, race or background. Believers cannot be identified with certainty by the denominations to which they belong or the badges they may choose to wear. But we cannot spend long together before we are able to identify those who truly know the Father and the Son. Christian fellowship has a tremendous potential for joy because at its core is sharing what our individual fellowship with God means, and what he has taught us. When the going is tough, that fellowship brings all the greater joy because it provides strength and support. The final chapter of the Acts of the Apostles records Paul's journey as a prisoner to Rome. He had no idea what awaited him as he stood trial. Christians in Rome, however, whom he had never met, heard of his proximity to the city. At two points on his route, they went out to meet and welcome him. Little wonder Luke wrote, 'At the sight of these men Paul thanked God and was encouraged' (28:15). Christian fellowship is 'a joy tonic' that raises our spirits.

Future and glorious prospects

Conditioned by our contemporary world to be preoccupied with the immediate here and now, an essential foundation of Christian joy is often missed — the joy of future and glorious prospects. Take, for instance, Romans 5:2-5: 'And we rejoice in the hope of the glory of God. Not only so, but we also rejoice in our sufferings, because we know that suffering produces perseverance; perseverance, character; and character, hope. And hope does not disappoint us, because God has poured out his love into our hearts by the Holy Spirit, whom he has given us.' The hope God places before us is sharing our Lord Jesus Christ's glory and participating in his triumph. The Lord Jesus specifically asked his Father, 'Father, I want those you have given me to be with me where I am, and to see my glory, the glory you have given me because you loved me before the creation of the world' (John 17:24). Indispensable to the joy set before him as he endured the cross was the prospect of our joining him in glory and sharing his triumph.

Seldom can joy be known in any sphere or context if hope is absent. This explains the frequent absence of genuine joy in our contemporary world. Experience indicates that we tend to think and speak all too little of our hope, whether in talking about the Lord Jesus himself, who is our hope, or of the hope he inspires and guarantees of eternal glory. We do not, or ought not, to look for all the good things now, but they are promised us in the life to come. When our bodies are beset by disease — and sometimes incurably so — and when our best human hopes are dashed to the ground, immense joy may be ours as we look forward to our corruptible bodies being changed and transformed so that they will be like our Saviour's glorious body (Philippians 3:21), wonderfully suited for an eternity with him.

A definition not to be missed

In our struggle to define Christian joy adequately, we must not miss the most important New Testament definition and description of joy — it is the joy of the Lord Jesus Christ himself in us. Shortly before his death on the cross, the Lord Jesus explained to his disciples that a principal purpose of his final conversations with them was that 'my joy may be in you and that your joy may be complete' (John 15:11; see also vv. 9 and 10). The importance of this needs to be pondered for it has breathtaking implications.

The Lord Jesus possessed a full and unique joy. No one ever knew so much opposition from Satan and the powers of evil, but these did not diminish his joy. No one faced such indescribable suffering as he did as he became the propitiation for our sins; but the joy of hope sustained him. He endured the cross, despising the shame for the joy that was set before him (Hebrews 12:2). His joy expressed itself in spontaneous praise and thanksgiving to his Father (Luke 10:21) and delight in his Father's will (John 4:34; cf. Psalm 40:8). Significantly, since our subject is the fruit of the Spirit, he was 'full of joy *through the Holy Spirit*' (Luke 10:21). The Holy Spirit communicated joy to him, just as he may convey it to us. Christian joy at its best is the Lord Jesus sharing his joy with us to the full as he shares our life (Revelation 3:20).

Joy's expression

Joy's expression is multi-faceted. Like a jewel held up to the light, it holds dazzling surprises. It does not despise the ordinary.

It enhances our pleasure of everyday things, since our new birth brings about a new appreciation of God's gifts. We recognize him as the source and author of all that is good (James 1:17). Everything he created is good and is to be received with thanksgiving (1 Timothy 4:4), since he has provided them for our enjoyment (1 Timothy 6:17). We find reasons for joy and gladness in most ordinary things as we recognize them as God's gifts (Acts 2:46). We have eyes to see creation as 'the theatre of God's glory',[2] upon the stage of which we see God's amazing goodness and generosity. As someone has aptly said, the psalmists have 'season tickets in the theatre'.[3]

Fresh appreciation of creation

Christian joy brings a new appreciation and pleasure in everything God has created. This is the uniform testimony of believers in every generation. In many of the psalms David expresses his appreciation. Take, for example, Psalm 19:

> The heavens declare the glory of God;
>> the skies proclaim the work of his hands.
> Day after day they pour forth speech;
>> night after night they display knowledge.
> There is no speech or language
>> where their voice is not heard.
> Their voice goes out into all the earth,
>> their words to the ends of the world.
>
> In the heavens he has pitched a tent for the sun,
>> which is like a bridegroom coming forth from his pavilion,
>> like a champion rejoicing to run his course.
> It rises at one end of the heavens
>> and makes its circuit to the other;
>> nothing is hidden from its heat
>
>   (vv. 1-6).

In the early eighteenth century Jonathan Edwards described the beginning of his new life as a Christian:

> After this my sense of divine things gradually increased, and became more and more lively, and had more of that inward sweetness. The appearance of everything was altered; there seemed to be, as it were, a calm, sweet cast, or appearance of divine glory, in almost every thing. God's excellency, his wisdom, his purity and love, seemed to appear in everything; in the sun, moon, and stars; in the clouds, and blue sky; in the grass, flowers, trees; in the water, and all nature; which used greatly to fix my mind. I often used to sit and view the moon for continuance; and in the day, spent much time in viewing the clouds and sky, to behold the sweet glory of God in these things...[4]

Jonathan Edwards' testimony is especially interesting because he goes on to say that as he looked at God's creation in a new way, he found himself:

> mean time, singing forth, with a low voice my contemplations of the Creator and Redeemer... While thus engaged, it always seemed natural to me to sing, or chant for my meditations; or, to speak my thoughts in soliloquies with a singing voice.[5]

Praise and worship

Joy finds voice in praise and thanksgiving, often in singing, as the Holy Spirit aids that expression through psalms, hymns and spiritual songs (Ephesians 5:18-20). As we have been made right with God through his Son, we feel it appropriate to urge one another:

> Sing joyfully to the LORD, you righteous;
>   it is fitting for the upright to praise him
>
>   (Psalm 33:1).

Before our conversion, we may never have enjoyed singing, but since then we have never ceased to find joy in praising and thanking God in song, especially with other believers. I have found it particularly encouraging to see a man singing in a church service for the first time. For months, since first coming to church, he has refrained from singing, almost conspicuously so. Singing had only been his habit when in the pub or at a football match. But now, wonderfully, he has been converted and he shows it by singing!

Confidence in God

Joy expresses itself in confidence in God and in his supplies of strength (Nehemiah 8:10). William Grimshaw exercised a significant ministry in Haworth, Yorkshire, in the eighteenth century, in spite of considerable opposition and difficulties. Henry Venn, a well-known Christian at the time, said of him, 'His very countenance proclaimed that the joy of the Lord was his strength.' Grimshaw himself said, 'The true Christian ... is well-provided for both worlds. He is sure of peace here and glory above and therefore enjoys a light heart and a cheerful face.'[6]

Rejoices in persecution

Joy not only survives difficult circumstances but sometimes seems to thrive on them. It rejoices in persecution as it focuses on the reward the Lord Jesus promises faithful disciples (Matthew 5:12) and the privilege of being counted worthy of suffering disgrace for his name (Acts 5:41). The Spirit, whose fruit this joy is, gives strength to endure joyfully (Colossians 1:11-12), especially as he gives insight to the harvest our trials and sufferings may produce in perseverance (Romans 5:3; James 1:2-3), righteousness and peace (Hebrews 12:11), and the development of the character of our Lord Jesus in us, as we allow ourselves to be trained by them.

Delights in fellowship

Joy finds expression in confident prayer and delight in fellowship with God. On the night he was betrayed, the Lord Jesus promised his disciples, 'Until now you have not asked for anything in my name. Ask and you will receive, and your joy will be complete' (John 16:24). The apostle John identified this glorious fellowship with God, and the fellowship it gives us with one another, as a great wonder of our redemption. He wrote, 'We proclaim to you what we have seen and heard, so that you also may have fellowship with us. And our fellowship is with the Father and with his Son, Jesus Christ. We write this to make our joy complete' (1 John 1:3-4).

Jonathan Edwards' testimony was that his joy found expression in fellowship with God by prayer. He wrote, 'I was almost constantly in ejaculatory prayer, wherever I was. Prayer seemed to be natural to me, as the breath by which the inward burnings of my heart had vent.'[7]

Gives generously

Joy expresses itself in generous giving. By nature, some are more generous than others. Through new birth, however, all believers, as they grow spiritually, increase in generosity. The explanation is simple: when we receive the grace of the Lord Jesus in salvation, it works within us making us more like our heavenly Father. The joy God gives us in his Son is an 'overflowing joy', and it wells up 'in rich generosity' as we become aware of the needs of others (2 Corinthians 8:2). Christian joy prompts us to give as much as we are able, and beyond our ability (2 Corinthians 8:3; cf. Mark 12:41-44). Generosity does not need human prompting or urging where joy is its spring.

A question that must be addressed

How does the fruit of the Spirit as joy relate to the common human problem of depression? Does the Spirit's joy mean that Christians should never be depressed? The reason for asking such questions is that Christians who suffer from depression, in its different forms, may find themselves feeling guilty, and often quite wrongly so. Any attempt to answer these questions demands recognition of important factors.

1. *We are different temperamentally.* Some possess cheerful dispositions, whereas others are more disposed to be sad or despondent. Some are inclined to be hopeful, and others always anticipate the worse. It is imperative that we recognize that some are more liable to depression since our natural temperaments are not changed by our new birth, our regeneration. The disposition we had before we became Christians will tend to characterize us now. If we were inclined to depression before conversion, that tendency will remain, much as it may be corrected and counteracted by our experience of God's grace.

2. *Depression may often result from physical causes over which we have little control.* Medication prescribed for physical ailments sometimes has a depressive effect. Post-natal depression clearly results from physical causes.

3. *All believers may lose their joy at times.* The book of Psalms illustrates this (for example, Psalms 42 and 43), as does Christian biography. Admittedly, this may sometimes be through sin, as David indicates in Psalm 51, where, having sinned grievously, he cries to God for the restoration of the joy of God's salvation (v. 12). However, it is clear elsewhere in the book of Psalms that believers experience depression sometimes through no fault of their own and often discover rich treasures of darkness through dark periods of the soul.

4. *If we are spiritually depressed, it is appropriate to ask ourselves, and God, as we pray, 'Is there a spiritual reason for this? Have I done something that spoils my spiritual joy?'* We may be sure that the Holy Spirit will, through our conscience and the application of his Word, show us the cause if this is the reason. If he does not, we must then persevere, and trust God, knowing that it is one of those 'all things' God allows in our lives that he will turn to spiritual good, in his own time. We must regard depression as we would any other human illness or ailment, recognizing that faith in God and being a Christian do not exempt us from the common problems and challenges of life.

5. *Whatever our natural temperament, it is clear that Christian joy, the joy that is part of the Spirit's fruit, has a remarkably positive effect for good upon our well-being, whatever our natural temperament.* As the body affects the soul, so the soul may have an impact upon the body. As our natural temperament may inhibit joy, so the well-being of our soul may help to overcome weaknesses of temperament. Some of us are natural worriers compared with others who are much more 'laid-back' and unaffected by circumstances. In other words, a deficiency in our temperament may be helped by the Spirit's indwelling presence as he teaches us the way to joy, and not least through fellowship with God in prayer.

Christian joy is not a matter of temperament but it is intended by God to be the expression of living faith in him. A dominant figure in the early history of the Scripture Union, or Children's Special Service Mission as it was then known, was Tom Bishop. By nature, he was a pessimist and full of forebodings for the future of the mission. One of his colleagues records that frequently he saw him enter the office downcast and gloomy, 'and then he used to kneel down at the office table and pray, and get up with the creases out of his forehead'. It is the undoubted testimony of many Christians that issues, problems and difficulties that used to lead them into depression are replaced by spiritual joy as they turn to God in prayer and find his peace that passes all human understanding.

Maintaining our joy

While uniquely the gift of the Holy Spirit, we have a part to play in the maintenance of our joy. There is no doubt that God intends it should be maintained for we are urged to 'Be joyful always' (1 Thessalonians 5:16). Outward or physical trials and difficulties that affect ordinary human happiness should make no difference since the one in whom our joys are found is always the same (1 Peter 1:6; Hebrews 13:8). Like Habakkuk in desperate times we can declare:

> Though the fig-tree does not bud
>   and there are no grapes on the vines,
> though the olive crop fails
>   and the fields produce no food,
> though there are no sheep in the pen
>   and no cattle in the stalls,
> yet I will rejoice in the LORD,
>   I will be joyful in God my Saviour
>
> (3:17-18).

David put it well when he wrote,

I said to the LORD, 'You are my Lord;
    apart from you I have no good thing'
                                        (Psalm 16:2).

He would have agreed with the joy Asaph expressed:

Whom have I in heaven but you?
    And earth has nothing I desire besides you.
My flesh and my heart may fail,
    but God is the strength of my heart
    and my portion for ever
                                        (Psalm 73:25-26).

Paul wrote of being 'sorrowful, yet always rejoicing; poor, yet making many rich; having nothing, and yet possessing everything' (2 Corinthians 6:10).

In the sixth century Columba, known as the apostle of Scotland, went to Iona. He left behind a tradition of godliness and holiness. It is written of him that 'in the midst of all his cares he showed himself open and friendly to everyone; he bore the joy of the Holy Spirit in the inmost places of his heart'.[8] The consistency of Christian testimony to the power of the Spirit's joy throughout all the centuries is wonderful in its encouragement.

How to maintain joy

Watchfulness

The maintenance of our joy requires, first, watchfulness. Since a joyless Christian has little testimony to give, the enemy of our souls aims to remove our joy. He does so by surreptitiously encouraging us to neglect practical righteousness. If we close our eyes and ears to moral and social obligations, whether within our families or those outside of them, we lose our joy. Fulness of joy comes to 'those who hunger and thirst for righteousness' (Matthew 5:6).

Not taking the trouble to seek peace in human relationships is a similar peril. Fulness of joy comes to the peacemakers (Matthew 5:9). Everything that grieves the Holy Spirit is to be guarded against, since his ministry is the key to our experience of the Saviour's joy. Particular dangers to guard against are unbelief (Philippians 1:25; 1 Peter 1:6-7), disobedience (John 15:10-11), neglect of prayer (John 16:24), broken fellowship with God and his people, and unconfessed sin (Psalm 51:3, 8, 9, 12; 1 John 1:1-10).

A positive attitude

Along with watchfulness, and equally important, is a positive or proactive attitude to our Christian life. We are to build on what God has given us. Since the faith God has given us is a gift, we may be tempted to take it for granted, whereas we need to determine to grow in faith. Progress in faith leads to joy in the faith (Philippians 1:25). The same may be said of our hope. Although given us by God as 'living hope', it demands to be cultivated. Someone may make us a gift of a young and healthy plant. To see its fruit appear, however, we must water it and care for it.

Every Sunday as we celebrate the resurrection of our Lord Jesus, we should remind ourselves of the victory over death we have in him, the certainty of our own resurrection and transformation, and the inheritance kept in heaven for us that can never perish, spoil or fade (1 Peter 1:3-4). Our Saviour is to return. Our bodies, if dead, are to be raised. We are to be with him where he is, and we are to see his glory. As our hope overflows,

so will our joy (Romans 15:13). When our joy is disturbed by
the harsh realities of serious illness and death, then is the time
to listen afresh to our Saviour's words that enable us to find joy
in the face of them all (John 14:1-4).

Prayer

When our joy is threatened by worry, we should carefully pray
about all that gives us concern, not neglecting to pray about the
small things as well as the big. Prayer is the irreplaceable instrument by which we look to God and are made radiant (Psalm
34:5; John 16:24). Every time we pray it is good to recall afresh
the privilege of fellowship with God the Father and the Son as
they make their home with us by the Holy Spirit living within
us. An important aspect of prayer is spending time turning over
in our minds the attributes of God, especially as they are displayed in his Son. Joy's radiance is enhanced by the peace that
praying about everything, with thanksgiving, brings to our hearts
and minds as they rest afresh in our spiritual union with our
Saviour and our Father's perfect care (Philippians 4:6-7).

Listening to the Spirit

Since the Holy Spirit imparts our joy in God and in his Son, our
top priority must be to neither grieve nor quench him. We quench
him by not listening to his voice and we grieve him by spoiling
our relationship with God through disobedience. Whenever we
lack joy, we must examine whether we are listening and being
obedient to him. To be filled with the Spirit is to be filled with
joy (Acts 13:52). Filled with the Spirit, we speak 'to one another with psalms, hymns and spiritual songs'. We 'sing and
make music in [our] heart to the Lord, always giving thanks to
God the Father for everything, in the name of our Lord Jesus
Christ' (Ephesians 5:18-20).

The best joy is before us

'Joy is the serious business of heaven,' wrote C. S. Lewis.[9] The Lord Jesus spoke about the joy in heaven over one sinner coming to repentance. How great will be our joy when we are finally gathered into our heavenly home with our Saviour! Peter wrote of Christians being 'filled with an inexpressible and glorious joy' although we have not yet seen him. How inexpressible and glorious our joy will be when we do see him! (1 Peter 1:8). The joy we now know is a foretaste of what is to come!

Essential to Christian witness

Christian joy is an essential part of our witness in the world. In the 1960s when journalists assessed the influence of the personalities of that period, and especially of the pop groups, they put *The Beatles* at the top of the list. Significantly, they did so because 'their influence is not only felt through their songs, but through their combination of individualism, solidarity and unmistakable sense of joy'.[10] As Christian believers we deserve rebuke if an 'unmistakable sense of joy' is absent from our lives.

People may be more prompted to think about our Lord Jesus Christ by our joy than by our words. The evidence of first-century history is that the joyful enthusiasm of the early Christians added weight to the unashamed claims they made for the Lord Jesus Christ as the Son of God and only Saviour. Even in prison for his sake, they were able to sing his praise. Conversion and joy went together (Acts 8:8; 13:52; 15:3). Exuberant joy is one of the most powerful factors in the spread of the gospel. Therefore, guard your joy — your joy in the Lord!

4.

Peace

The first, or Christian, names we possess tend to vary according to the period in which we were born. A favourite of a former generation was Irene, chosen often because of its original meaning. It is the Greek translation of the Hebrew word *Shalom*. *Shalom* means everything that makes for a person's good and well-being.

When we use the word 'peace' we invariably think in personal, if not selfish, terms of our enjoyment of peace. Many blessings from God have a corporate as much as a personal aspect and this is certainly the case with peace.

Eirene can mean the personal experience of peace as in Philippians 4:7, what we may describe as peace of soul; and most certainly the most important peace — peace with God as in Romans 5:1. But here in the fruit of the Spirit it has to do with our relationships to others, as when Paul urges: 'Live in peace with each other' (1 Thessalonians 5:13). The same Bible word *eirene* has to be interpreted according to its context. Let me explain, therefore, why I opt for *peaceableness* — or *peace-loving* — rather than peace.

1. All other aspects of the fruit of the Spirit relate to our behaviour and relationships with others. We might at first

think that joy is an exception but we saw earlier that fulness
of joy comes to peacemakers (Matthew 5:9).

2. It is the reflection and reproduction in us of God's character
   as we see it so wonderfully displayed in our Lord Jesus. He
   came to make peace, and to enable us to live in peace with
   others.

3. To translate it as *peaceableness* accords with other passages
   where *eirene* is plainly used in this sense, as when Paul urges
   the believers in Rome: 'If it is possible, as far as it depends
   on you, live at peace with everyone' (Romans 12:18); and
   later reminds them: 'The kingdom of God is not a matter of
   eating and drinking, but of righteousness, peace and joy in
   the Holy Spirit' (Romans 14:17). In the context this meant
   that Christians should not squabble over what they should
   eat and drink. This peace is the opposite of strife, conflict
   and quarrels (James 4:1), and is a peace to be actively
   pursued (2 Timothy 2:22; Romans 14:19), to be kept rather
   than broken, a fruit of the wisdom that God uniquely gives
   (James 3:17). However, there is a fundamental link between
   peace and peaceableness, since the latter is a direct
   consequence of the discovery of peace with God through
   our Lord Jesus Christ.

The priority of peace with God

The world demonstrably lacks peace. Wherever we live, and
wherever we look in the human race, we note its absence. In
the last six thousand years there has not been a single year
without a war somewhere. In the last three hundred years there
have been more than three hundred and eighty-six wars in
Europe. Since 1500, more than eight thousand known peace

treaties have been agreed. Each was signed with the intention that it should last for ever, and yet their average length is little over two years. The root cause is the same everywhere — human sin. '"There is no peace," says the Lord, "for the wicked"' (Isaiah 48:22; 57:21). While 'wicked' is an adjective we commonly reserve for the worst possible crimes, in the Bible it describes all who are guilty of sin against God and their fellow human beings. Rebellious, fallen human beings do not know the way of peace (Romans 3:17).

The source of genuine happiness

When we lack peace, genuine happiness and prosperity are elusive because they cannot be enjoyed without it (Lamentations 3:17). God our Creator is the proper source of our safety and security (Psalm 4:8; cf. 91:1). Without him, we cannot find them. Here is the crux of the human problem. Having alienated ourselves from him by our sin, we have forfeited his gift of peace. Nothing we do can remedy the tragedy.

Provided by his own Son

God's unique solution was the incarnation and atoning death of his Son to be the one Mediator between himself and us. A mediator is, literally, a go-between. He mediates between two parties to produce peace by removing disagreement. Peace with God is possible only as the demands of his just wrath against our sins are satisfied. God made this possible by the atoning death of his Son at Calvary. The Bible expresses it clearly: 'For God was pleased to have all his fulness dwell in him, and through him to reconcile to himself all things, whether things on earth or things in heaven, by making peace through his blood, shed on the cross' (Colossians 1:19-20). The Lord Jesus Christ came to guide our feet into the way of peace (Luke 1:79). His saving work is the sole foundation for our peace with God (Ephesians 2:14-17).

Repentance towards God and faith in Jesus Christ as Saviour and Lord are God's door for us to enter into his peace. This peace follows immediately upon the heels of faith in his Son. As men and women believed in the Lord Jesus Christ during his ministry, he tellingly said to them, 'Go in peace' (Mark 5:34; Luke 7:50). So it is with us, for, as Paul concludes, 'Since we have been justified through faith, we have peace with God through our Lord Jesus Christ' (Romans 5:1). *The Lord Jesus himself is our peace* (Ephesians 2:14). He, its Guarantor and Guardian, can give it at all times and in every way (2 Thessalonians 3:16). Peace is inseparable therefore from the experience of God's grace in Christ (Galatians 1:3; 1 Thessalonians 1:1). Grace and peace go together and always in that order. Peace is God's gift and he delights in our enjoyment of it (Psalm 29:11).

A peace that is unique

The peace God gives through his Son is different from the peace the world sometimes knows, for it can uniquely quieten our hearts when we feel most troubled and afraid. The Lord Jesus had no material possessions to leave his disciples but he bequeathed them peace (John 14:27), a peace that surpasses human understanding (Philippians 4:7). Of all the pictures portraying peace, two are particularly meaningful. In the Old Testament God's peace is likened to *a river* (Isaiah 48:18), a way of saying that it is not a seasonal stream but an ever-flowing resource. In the New Testament it is compared to *a sentry* in that it guards our hearts against all that threatens to disturb them (Philippians 4:7).

While God's peace through our Lord Jesus Christ is a gift, once we possess it three keys to our enjoyment of it stand out.

1. *Our obedience to God* (Psalm 119:165). A consequence of salvation is obedience to our Lord Jesus Christ by which the Spirit's sanctifying work progresses in our lives (1 Peter 1:2).

2. *The pursuit of righteousness* (that is to say, a right relationship with God and the active pursuit of right that proceeds from it), the expected consequence of obedience. Peace and righteousness are in such harmony that they may be said to 'kiss each other' (Psalm 85:10; cf. Isaiah 48:18). They are partners.

3. *Daily fellowship with God,* especially by prayer (Philippians 4:6-7).

   Bethan Lloyd-Jones described her experience as a young mother when her husband was away from home. They lived close to the coast in Wales, and one night there was an exceptionally severe gale blowing in from the sea. 'I lay,' she wrote, 'beside myself with fear, tossing feverishly in bed, full of terror and panic — if the tide came up Victoria Road, could I escape with the baby? get out of the window? on to the roof? etc. At last, in sheer helpless despair, I got out of bed and on to my knees, and I prayed: "Lord, if it is all true, if you are really there and will answer my prayer, *please* give me peace and take all my fear away." As I spoke, it all went away, my heart was flooded with perfect peace, and I never had any more fear of gales and tides. I was completely delivered and asleep in two minutes.'[1] Prayer can calm the most disturbed mind.

Peaceableness

What we have established about peace with God is fundamental to understanding peaceableness. The peace we know *with* God, and *from* God, requires us to be at peace with one another, since this was one of the purposes for which our Lord Jesus Christ died (Ephesians 2:14). Peaceableness has an international application. We find in the Lord Jesus a meeting place and harmony with fellow-believers, regardless of what may have been our previous divisions of race, colour, class or circumstance (Ephesians 2:14-18). Unhelpful and sinful attitudes to people whose backgrounds are different, and even opposed to our own, disappear as the Spirit's fruit grows in us.

Creates harmony

Peaceableness is the oil that makes human relationships harmonious. Think of what happens when oil is absent from machinery. Soon there will be friction, noise and then breakdown. So it is in human relationships. To change the picture, peaceableness is a direct consequence of having the salt of the gospel in our life (Mark 9:50). As salt acts as a preservative, so our influence in society should contribute to preserve peace and harmony. Peaceableness makes us constructive rather than destructive in our influence upon others (Romans 14:17-19).

Outworking of love

Peaceableness is the natural outworking of love, the primary aspect of the Spirit's fruit: love is not easily provoked (1 Corinthians 13:4-5). As our Lord Jesus Christ's peace rules in our hearts, we recognize his call to live in peace (Colossians 3:15; 1 Thessalonians 5:13). Peaceableness becomes an objective to which we set our minds. Whenever we ask for wisdom from God in handling human relationships, his answer is always insight that enables us to be peace-loving and peace-makers (James 3:17-18). Even when God disciplines us, an experience seldom pleasant, one of his purposes is to produce peaceableness in our characters (Hebrews 12:11), so that we discover the blessing the Lord Jesus promised to peacemakers of being identified as God's children (Matthew 5:9).

Peaceableness in practice

Peace with everyone

Peaceableness means making every effort to live in peace with everyone (Hebrews 12:14). Negatively, it is synonymous with avoiding foolish and stupid arguments and refusing to let resentment find a place in our heart (2 Timothy 2:23-24). Positively, it is synonymous with being kind, considerate, gentle, and respectful to everyone, always striving after fairness and lack of prejudice. The first expression of peaceableness must be in the home for:

Better a dry crust with peace and quiet
    than a house full of feasting, with strife
                                        (Proverbs 17:1).

It is to a life of peace that God has called us in marriage (1 Corinthians 7:15). The secret of peaceableness in marriage is the deliberate concentration of each partner upon his or her duties rather than what he or she may expect from the other as a matter of right (Ephesians 5:22, 25). For parents, peaceableness requires sensitivity and realism in their demands and expectations of their children. Fathers, for instance, are not to 'exasperate' their children (Ephesians 6:4), something that happens when demands made of them are unrealistic and unreasonable.

Within the church fellowship, peaceableness means consistently striving for peace and agreement (Colossians 3:15). It is
an axiom of church life that 'God is not a God of disorder but
of peace' (1 Corinthians 14:33). Every effort is to be made 'to
keep the unity of the Spirit through the bond of peace'
(Ephesians 4:3). Seldom, if ever, are those who hold office in
the church faultless as they carry out their tasks, and inevitably
room for criticism arises. The recognition, however, that Christian
love — the first aspect of the Spirit's fruit — demands that they
should be held 'in the highest regard in love because of their
work' (1 Thessalonians 5:13) motivates us to peaceableness
and careful handling of criticism. Some activities lead to peace,
and others — like following a secret or hidden agenda — do
not. We are to pursue those that lead to peace, and flee without
argument from those that do not (2 Timothy 2:22).

Our desire for peace is to extend to all human relationships.
If it is possible, as far as it depends upon us, we are to 'live at
peace with everyone' (Romans 12:18).

Required of all

While it is easier temperamentally for some than for others,
peaceableness is an equal requirement of all Christians. At first,
considerable effort may be required, but as we make it our
consistent endeavour, it may become almost second nature.
Aspects of other people's characters can irritate and annoy us
— and often understandably, since we may not be the only
ones who react in that way. But every time we act peaceably,
we sow good seeds that result in more harmonious relationships and less irritation (James 3:18). Peaceableness enables
us to focus upon people's good points rather than their bad
habits. This helps to bring the best out of them, with rewarding
consequences.

In words and actions

While actions have much to contribute to peaceableness, words often have more. The book of Proverbs contains a blunt description of people whose words are not peaceable:

> A fool's lips bring him strife,
>   and his mouth invites a beating.
> A fool's mouth is his undoing,
>   and his lips are a snare to his soul
>
> (18:6-7).

Nowhere are the dangers of the tongue better expressed than in James 3 where James stresses the difficulty of taming the tongue (3:1-12). As powerful as a bit in the mouth of a horse (v. 3), or a small rudder that steers a large ship (v. 4), the tongue can either enflame or dampen strife. It can either promote or destroy peace:

> A gentle answer turns away wrath,
>   but a harsh word stirs up anger
>   (Proverbs 15:1; cf. 17:27).

Peaceable speech requires us to recognize that there are times when it is best for words to be few (Proverbs 11:12-13).

Relinquishing our own rights

Sometimes the achievement of peace calls for the relinquishing of our rights, although that does not mean pretending problems do not exist but rather determining to deal with them peaceably (Genesis 21:22-32; 26:12-25). If before ever we raise an issue we decide that we will not let it get out of hand, we will

find ourselves more than halfway to success. James Guthrie, a
contemporary of Samuel Rutherford, would often say if tempers
became frayed over a matter under discussion, 'Enough of this,
let us go on to some other subject, we are warm and can dispute no longer with advantage.'[2]

Taking the first steps

Peaceableness sometimes requires us to take initiative in coming
between contending parties in order to make peace (Matthew
5:9). Abigail's example is to be emulated (1 Samuel 25:18-35).
She was the peace-loving wife of a belligerent husband who
had failed to exercise the reciprocal hospitality and kindness to
which David was entitled. As soon as Abigail discovered this
failure, she took initiative to rectify and ease the crisis by
making up for her husband's lapse and folly. Her action not
only saved bitter disagreement but also averted bloodshed.
Sometimes our efforts may fail, but the effort is nevertheless
necessary.

William Grimshaw, an eighteenth-century minister in
Haworth, Yorkshire, was an outstanding peacemaker. Nothing
was too much trouble for him in his attempts to make peace
between people. He was known to fall down on his knees before them, urging them, for the sake of the Lord Jesus, to love
one another.

The examples we have given are not to lead us to the conclusion that God requires us to seek peace at any price, no
matter what the issue may be. Undoubted sin, false teaching
and behaviour that plainly dishonour the Lord Jesus Christ must
be confronted and remedied where possible. Some examples
to help us in this can be found in the New Testament. Much as
Paul loved the Corinthian church, he knew that the moral lapses
there, which had been passed over, had to be faced and taken

care of without delay (1 Corinthians 5:1-13). He greatly re-
spected the apostle Peter and his unique place among the
apostles, but when he behaved in a way that contradicted a
fundamental truth of the gospel, Paul had to rebuke him face to
face (Galatians 2:14).

Our priority concern must be the spirit in which we confront
difficult issues. Sadly, it is possible to love controversy and to
find pleasure in rebuking wrong. None who enjoy it should
engage in it. The confrontation of wrong and the exercise of
church discipline need to be done with integrity so that the two-
fold aim is the honour of God and the spiritual well-being and
good of all involved. When error, sin and misdeeds are properly dealt with, in the spirit of Christ, peace — and not further
disharmony — is promoted.

Peaceableness as a priority

Since God is slow to anger (Nehemiah 9:17; Psalm 103:8; Jonah
4:2), his children are to be the same. The peaceableness of our
Lord Jesus Christ was prophesied and emphasized in the Old
Testament (Zechariah 9:9) and amply fulfilled when he came
(Matthew 21:4-5; John 12:14-15). His peaceableness is something we are actively called to follow, even under the most severe
provocation (1 Peter 2:21-23).

Personal benefits

Peaceableness brings immeasurable benefits to personal well-
being. Spiritual joy is vitally linked with the pursuit of righteousness and peace (Romans 14:17). When the cost of pursuing
peace is at its most demanding, our joy may also be at its peak.
Joy and peace are inseparable twins. With love, they are
inseparable triplets.

Contemporary society studies and practises psychosomatic medicine out of the recognition that physical symptoms of illness are sometimes caused by worry or unhappiness rather than deep-seated physical problems. Centuries before the term 'psychosomatic medicine' was used, the book of Proverbs established that 'A heart at peace gives life to the body' (Proverbs 14:30). It is no hardship to strive to be at peace with everyone since it can only bring us total good, not least because it is one of the conditions of God's presence and blessing upon us. Having urged the Corinthians to be of one mind and to live in peace, Paul immediately adds: 'And the God of love and peace will be with you' (2 Corinthians 13:11). What we may sometimes feel we lose or forfeit through striving to preserve neighbourly peace, we will often discover God making up to us in his Spirit's peace (Genesis 13:14-18). We find ourselves inheriting a blessing (1 Peter 3:9) — no poor exchange!

Benefits for God's people

God's people benefit enormously where peaceableness rules. As they practise peace, they are able to function effectively as Christ's body (1 Corinthians 14:33). Spiritual edification and development require an environment of peace (Romans 14:19). Peaceableness makes us quick to notice potential differences, and speedy in mending broken fences. It is the binding power that helps us travel on the same road and in the same direction, so that we stay together not only in theory but also in practice (Ephesians 4:3).

Influences surprising outcomes

God sometimes employs peaceableness to win surprising victories, victories that might not have been won in any other way. An outstanding example at the end of the twentieth century was the influence of Nelson Mandela in bringing an end to apartheid in South Africa. In his autobiography he makes a telling comment: 'To make peace with an enemy, one must work with that enemy, and that enemy becomes your partner.'[3] Peaceableness may bring opponents to their senses and to a better understanding (1 Samuel 24:17), and make them ashamed of their wrongful actions (1 Peter 3:15-16). As in the case of Abigail (1 Samuel 25:18-35), it may provide a way of escape from a potentially horrendous state of affairs.

The New Testament urges us no less than the Old to 'seek peace and pursue it' if we are to 'love life and see good days' (1 Peter 3:10-11). Such advice is not only good because it has stood the test of time but it is also divine wisdom. A delightful promise in the book of Psalms is a great encouragement: 'There is a future for the man of peace' (Psalm 37:37). James assures us that 'Peacemakers who sow in peace raise a harvest of right-eousness' (James 3:18).

Questions to ask and practical action

- Will our lives produce a harvest of righteousness?
- Are we prepared to set our minds towards peaceableness? We can liken the setting of our minds towards it like the setting of sails on a yacht. I know little about yachting but there are certain things that are clear. First, you must know where you want to go. Second, you must recognize your dependence upon the wind. Third, you must set your sails accordingly.

    The direction in which we want to go is towards peaceable-ness. We must recognize our dependence upon the wind of the Spirit. As we set our sails aright, we will achieve our goal.

- Are there particular people who challenge us to be peaceable?
- Will we now commit ourselves to pray for them and for ourselves in our reactions towards them?
- Will we resolve to aim to be at peace with everyone?
- If our answer is 'yes', it must be in dependence upon our Lord Jesus Christ and his Spirit's help.
- As we plant seeds of peace, we will produce a harvest of goodness and righteousness.

5.

Patience

The Spirit's fruit is a perfectly balanced whole. Each part is in complete harmony with the rest. Patience probably follows peace or peaceableness in Paul's list since the latter cannot be achieved without the practice of patience. Impatience never contributes peace to human relationships. Again, the first aspect of the Spirit's fruit — love — influences and controls the rest, since one of its foremost expressions is patience.

Two Greek words are used for patience in the New Testament: the first relates chiefly to circumstances, and the second more to people. The first expresses the quality that neither surrenders to difficulties nor gives way under trial. It is the opposite of despondency and is associated with hope. It is, however, seldom used of God. The second word describes self-restraint that does not retaliate or hastily punish in the face of provocation. It is the opposite of anger, and is associated with mercy. Used of God, it is the word chosen to describe this aspect of the Spirit's fruit. It may sometimes be expressed as forbearance and steadfastness.

The literal meaning of the Greek word translated here as patience is 'long-temperedness'. We sometimes refer to someone as being short-tempered. A travel writer met an Indian author in Delhi whom he describes as 'an angry man'. He

writes, 'Over the hours I spent with him, he spluttered and
spat like a well-warmed frying pan.'[1] That well describes short-
temperedness. Long-temperedness, by contrast, puts anger —
that may be legitimate — on a slow cooker, so that it does not
boil over. The Bible uses both words for patience, and God
requires us to practise both aspects.

God's patience

God's patience is the proper place to begin since he is the God
of patience (Romans 15:5).

In the Old Testament

Patience, especially when revealed in slowness to anger, was
an essential element of God's self-revelation to his people in
the Old Testament. He put his protecting mark on Cain (Genesis 4:15) and gave the sign of the rainbow to a world that had
displayed its rebellion (Genesis 9:11-17; 1 Peter 3:20) — amazing displays of patience. His slowness to anger was vital to his
self-disclosure to Moses (Exodus 34:6; Numbers 14:18).

As the Jews reflected on their past and God's dealings with
them, they marvelled at his unfailing patience and kindness to
them (Nehemiah 9:30). Time and time again 'The Israelites did
evil in the eyes of the LORD; they forgot the LORD their God and
served the Baals and the Asherahs' (Judges 3:7). God's righteous anger then burned against them and he sold them into
the hands of their enemies, so that they were subject to them
(3:8). This was to discipline them, as parents discipline their
children. 'But when they cried out to the LORD, he raised up for
them a deliverer' (3:9). Sadly, the whole process soon began all
over again (3:12-15), but still God was patient with them. Hosea,
Amos and Jonah in particular give testimony to God's patience,

something God taught them to reproduce in their own characters (Hosea 2:14-23; Amos 4:6-11; Jonah 4:2). Jonah found it especially hard to learn, but learn it he had to, and did.

In the New Testament

God's patience became an assured or fail-safe truth among the Jews (Hosea 11:8-9), the outflow of his grace, compassion and love. The New Testament adds its own testimony. Here the emphasis is upon God's patience in giving men and women opportunity for repentance by delaying his righteous judgement upon them (2 Peter 3:15). Paul knew he was an outstanding example of such patience, for the encouragement of others (1 Timothy 1:16). Although he was at first a persecutor of Christians, God patiently worked in his life to bring him to faith in his Son. God's patience is seen in his willingness to wait and not to act immediately (1 Peter 3:20). He is rich in patience (Romans 2:4).

Gives opportunity for repentance

There is no conflict between God's patience and anger. In his patience he gives time and opportunity to men and women to come to that true repentance that will justify his anger's removal on the grounds of his Son's atoning death. If, however, a change does not take place, then wrath carries out its proper judgement and punishment (Numbers 14:18). His patience gives opportunity for the development of obedience or disobedience, deliverance or destruction (1 Peter 3:20). His anger's awesomeness necessarily increases the longer his patience receives no response (Romans 9:22). Since God waits to be gracious to us (Isaiah 30:18), his patience should lead us towards repentance (Romans 2:4). We, and everyone, are urged not to abuse his patience and the opportunity it gives of finding salvation (2 Peter 3:15).

We may sometimes find God's patience difficult to understand, particularly when his justice seems to be delayed. The
writers of the psalms wrestled with this problem (Psalm 35:17),
and none more than the writer of Psalm 73, as he envied the
prosperity of the wicked. His perplexity overwhelmed him until
he entered God's sanctuary, the temple. There God gave him
insight to understand their final destiny, causing him to declare:

> Surely you place them on slippery ground;
>   you cast them down to ruin.
> How suddenly are they destroyed,
>   completely swept away by terrors!
>
> (vv. 18-19).

A common cause of our wrestling with this problem is our human
concept of time (2 Peter 3:8). We do not see the end from the
beginning as God does, and we forget his almighty power and
certain justice.

Biblical examples of patience

Abraham, the prophets and Job provide the principal Old Testament examples of patience, and each presents a different focus.

Abraham

Abraham's patience meant waiting for the fulfilment of God's
promises to him — something he was not to see in his human
lifetime. God promised to bless him and make his descendants
'as numerous as the stars in the sky and the sand on the sea-
shore'. He assured him that through his offspring all nations on
earth would be blessed (Genesis 22:17-18). The long years
Abraham and Sarah waited for the conception and birth of

Isaac were a profound test of their patience. The lesson they learned was at some cost and not without mistakes on their part.

Many good things — and the best things — that God promises us are in the future, at our Lord's return. Patient waiting is required of us, just as it was of men and women of faith in the Old Testament. The writer to the Hebrews reminds us: 'All these people were still living by faith when they died. They did not receive the things promised; they only saw them and welcomed them from a distance. And they admitted that they were aliens and strangers on earth' (11:13). The patience required of them for what God promises in the future is the identical patience required of us (6:12).

The prophets

The example of the prophets was seen not only in their waiting for what God inspired them to prophesy, but also in their enduring, without resentment or rebellion, the suffering that speaking in his name brought (James 5:10). Commissioned by God and obedient to his call, they often suffered persecution and hardship. Elijah was hounded and hated (1 Kings 18:10, 17). Jeremiah was thrown into an empty water cistern with the threat of being starved to death (Jeremiah 38:1-13). Amos was falsely accused of 'raising a conspiracy' and told to go back to where he had come from (Amos 7:10-13).

In the Sermon on the Mount the Lord Jesus declares: 'Blessed are you when people insult you, persecute you and falsely say all kinds of evil against you because of me. Rejoice and be glad, because great is your reward in heaven, for in the same way they persecuted the prophets who were before you' (Matthew 5:11-12). Our characters — and especially our patience — are severely put to the test when, sure of God's will and purpose in what we do, we find ourselves ignored, despised and opposed. Trials are the fertilizers that cause patience to grow.

Patience cannot grow without circumstances that prompt impatience! George Muller was a wise pastor. A young man approached him with a spiritual problem. He said, 'Mr. Muller, my Christian life lacks patience. I wonder if you could show me how to find it?' George Muller told the young man that his problem was not too difficult to solve, and suggested that they both knelt in prayer. The pastor prayed, "Lord, I want you to give this young man some tribulation in his life. Give him weeks of tribulation; make that the experience of every day." The young man got up and pulled George Muller to his feet. "I am sorry, I think that you must have misunderstood me — it is patience that I want, not tribulation." "Indeed," said the pastor. "The Bible quite clearly says that 'tribulation worketh patience', so you won't find it in any other way."[2]

Job

Job's patience showed itself in dogged perseverance in the face of personal suffering and disaster (James 5:11). He would not have been the godly man that he was, and became, without the trials God permitted in his life. He suffered *materially* when all his worldly possessions were taken from him. He suffered *emotionally* when his sons and daughters were killed as the result of a hurricane and the collapse of the house in which they were feasting. He suffered *physically* as he was covered with painful sores from the soles of his feet to the top of his head. He suffered *mentally* as his wife encouraged him to abandon his faith in God, and as his friends showered their conflicting advice upon him. Yet he patiently endured and persevered.

In spite of all that the devil, the enemy of souls, threw at Job, he trusted God. 'Though he slay me, yet will I hope in

him,' he declared (Job 13:15). In the heat of the spiritual furnace
in which he found himself, Job exclaimed:

'I know that my Redeemer lives,
  and that in the end he will stand upon the earth.
And after my skin has been destroyed,
  yet in my flesh I will see God;
I myself will see him
  with my own eyes — I, and not another.
How my heart yearns within me!'

(19:25-27).

Job's patience in the severest possible trials proved the genuineness of his faith. Peter makes the same point: '…for a little
while you may have had to suffer grief in all kinds of trials.
These have come so that your faith — of greater worth than
gold, which perishes even though refined by fire — may be
proved genuine and may result in praise, glory and honour
when Jesus Christ is revealed' (1 Peter 1:6-7).

Let me take you back to 11 March 1812, to Serampore, not
far from Calcutta, where the first Baptist missionaries had settled in India, under the leadership of William Carey who, at the
age of fifty, had been in India nineteen years. He had worked
laboriously at language learning and Bible translation, and a
number of translation projects were in various stages of completion. William Ward, one of Carey's colleagues, was working
at his desk about six o'clock in the evening. Suddenly, he became aware of smoke seeping into his office. The paper store
was ablaze. All water had to be carried by hand. For four hours,
they fought the blaze. Ward left the group of fire fighters to
hurry back to his office to begin to remove the most valuable
papers. In his absence, someone had opened a window. The
consequent inrush of air caused the fire to flare into life. The

whole building was quickly engulfed in flames. How were they to tell Carey who was in Calcutta at the time of the fire? How to tell him that all his precious manuscripts were destroyed? The draft of his great polyglot dictionary; the Sikh and Telegu grammars; ten versions of the Bible that had been going through the press. When he was told, tears filled Carey's eyes. 'In one short evening,' he said, 'the labours of years are consumed. How unsearchable are the ways of God! I had lately brought some things to the utmost perfection of which they seemed capable, and contemplated the missionary establishment with perhaps too much self-congratulation. The Lord has laid me low, that I may look more simply to him.' But what then? 'With the doggedness which characterised his whole career, he patiently set to work to make his translations all over again. This time he brought to the work even greater dedication and utter humility...'[3]

The primary model

The foremost New Testament illustration of patience is our Lord Jesus Christ. Throughout the three years of his ministry, his patience with his disciples was extraordinary and unfailing. In spite of their slowness to understand (Mark 4:10-20), their worldly-mindedness (10:35-45) and their final desertion of him in his hour of need (Matthew 26:56; Mark 14:50; 16:7), he patiently persevered with them, loving them unceasingly until the end (John 13:1).

The supreme example of patience was his conduct during his trial and crucifixion (Matthew 26:59-68; 27:27-50). In the face of false witnesses, cruel violence and insult, he responded with patient submission to his Father's will. Peter witnessed this response and calls all believers to follow it:

To this you were called, because Christ suffered for you, leaving you an example, that you should follow in his steps.

'He committed no sin,
and no deceit was found in his mouth.'

When they hurled their insults at him, he did not retaliate; when he suffered, he made no threats. Instead, he entrusted himself to him who judges justly. He himself bore our sins in his body on the tree, so that we might die to sins and live for righteousness; by his wounds you have been healed. For you were like sheep going astray, but now you have returned to the Shepherd and Overseer of your souls

(1 Peter 2:21-25).

Essential to that righteousness, the outflow of the experience of salvation, is the exercise of patience, even under the severest provocation. Most of us find this a great challenge, especially when we recall how short a fuse our tempers often have. Patience demands that we deal with our anger, even when it is a righteous anger at wrongs done to us.

The patience Abraham revealed with regard to God's promises, the patience the prophets displayed in the face of opposition as they faithfully declared God's Word, and the patience Job showed under all kinds of physical, mental and spiritual suffering, find perfect exhibition in our Lord Jesus Christ. To be his follower or disciple is to walk in his footsteps here.

Following the pattern

Patience will often be tested by the most ordinary circumstances and challenges. Hudson Taylor, pioneer missionary to China, confessed: 'My greatest temptation is to lose my temper over the slackness and inefficiency so disappointing in those on whom I depended. It is no use to lose my temper — only kindness — but O, it is such a trial.'[4]

The model of God's dealings with us is to be the pattern of our interaction with others. A discerning pastor wrote to a church member who was serving abroad, 'It is a great mercy that God has far more patience with His people than any of His people have with each other.'[5] The patience and forbearance God has shown us are to be reproduced in our daily relationships with others. We will never need to be as patient with them as God has had to be with us.

The Lord Jesus related a telling story in which a man pleaded 'Be patient with me' and failed to get the response he ought to have received.

> The kingdom of heaven is like a king who wanted to settle accounts with his servants. As he began the settlement, a man who owed him ten thousand talents was brought to him. Since he was not able to pay, the master ordered that he and his wife and his children and all that he had be sold to repay the debt. The servant fell on his knees before him. 'Be *patient* with me,' he begged, 'and I will pay back everything.' The servant's master took pity on him, cancelled the debt and let him go. But when that servant went out, he found one of his fellow-servants who owed him a hundred denarii. He grabbed him and began to choke him. 'Pay back what you owe me!' he demanded. His fellow-servant fell to his knees and begged him, 'Be *patient* with me, and I will pay you back.' But he refused. Instead, he went off and had the man thrown into prison until he could pay the debt. When the other servants saw what had happened, they were greatly distressed and went and told their master everything that had happened. Then the master called the servant in. 'You wicked servant,' he said, 'I cancelled all that debt of yours because you begged me to. Shouldn't you have had mercy on your fellow-servant just as I had on you?' In anger his master turned him over to the jailers to be

tortured, until he should pay back all he owed. This is how my heavenly Father will treat each of you unless you forgive your brother from your heart

(Matthew 18:23-35).

Patience shown in forgiveness is the natural outflow of love. It is to be evident in *all* our relationships, whether we are warning, encouraging or helping others (1 Thessalonians 5:14).

Essential clothing

Using clothes as an illustration, the New Testament includes patience as a basic unisex spiritual garment — something we are to put on deliberately and feel ourselves undressed without (Colossians 3:12). Considerable patience is required if we are to teach others (2 Timothy 4:2). There is a Jewish saying, 'An irritable man cannot teach.' Patience is especially needed in leading and teaching young people, for so often they may seem indifferent to what we want them to understand. If we are to react properly to opposition to our Christian testimony, it is crucial to that testimony that we exercise patience and refuse to retaliate or feel sorry for ourselves (1 Peter 2:18-23; 3:13-14).

Patience brings its own rewards

We all know and love people who are not yet Christians. Their new birth and conversion may sometimes seem impossible. As God waited patiently for us to repent and believe on his Son, we too must be patient in our endeavours to win others to faith in him. Our confidence in God's sovereign power and the certainty that his Word will not return to him without fruit encourage us, even if we have to exercise patience for many years. As we persist in prayer and witness, many of them — if not all — may come to repentance and faith in our Lord Jesus Christ. It is helpful to remember how impossible our conversion may have seemed to some who were concerned for us before we came to faith.

Achieving patience

Patience does not happen by accident. It has to be our deliberate objective. To pray for it is appropriate because its achievement requires the injection of God's divine strength (Colossians 1:10-11). Furthermore, it is essential if we are to grow in the grace and knowledge of our Lord Jesus Christ. Patience may be thought of as a flower that God plants in our hearts at our new birth. As it grows there, it produces an attractive fragrance in our lives. As we pray about the matters that make us impatient, we find God helping us to see them in a proper perspective so that order and equilibrium are restored and we persevere in patience.

Practical action

- The most important goal is to focus our attention upon the example of our Lord Jesus Christ (Hebrews 12:1-3). Fixing our eyes on him is not only the secret of faith, but also the secret of patience.
- In what areas of life do we most require patience? As we iden-tify them, let us submit ourselves to God and his will in these areas.
- Are there people with whom we need to be especially patient?
- With our eyes upon our Lord Jesus Christ, let us determine to treat them as we know he treats both them and us.

6.

Kindness

I was intrigued. The National Library of Scotland in Edinburgh has most of its books catalogued on computer. Having typed in the word 'kindness' for books on the subject, the title that attracted my attention was a 282-page book, published in 1876 by Thomas Nelson, entitled *Kind words awaken kind echoes*, and subtitled 'Illustrations of the power of kindness'. There was no indication of the author's name in the edition I consulted. The introduction states: 'It is written as a humble but earnest recognition of the sacred maxim, "Let the same mind be in us as was in Christ."'

I wonder if such a book would be written today, or if it would find a publisher and a readership? The author's identification of kindness with the mind of the Lord Jesus in us is not only appropriate but also right up to date. The fruit of the Spirit is the reproduction in us of the character of our Saviour.

Kindness is love with its working clothes on, love in practice, doing good to others. The word itself is attractive, and brings to mind experiences that have been good and pleasant. Its appeal is increased when we consider the unappealing opposites with which it is contrasted in the New Testament — bitterness, anger, slander, malice, deceit, hypocrisy and envy.

Kindness is often linked with compassion, and follows it in 'the spiritual clothes' we are instructed to wear as proof that we are God's people (Colossians 3:12). It is almost synonymous with forgiveness of one another. Uninfluenced by the gratitude or ingratitude of those to whom it is extended, it does not stop when it receives nothing in return.

God's kindness the model

God is the ultimate example of kindness, a kindness he delights to exercise, especially in compassion. Often his kindness is expressed by the use of the word 'mercy'. His mercy, like his kindness, is his warm affection shown to the needy, helpless and distressed.

Kindness especially epitomizes his gracious acts and attitudes to sinners. In the delightful story of Ruth and Naomi, Naomi gave a significant testimony to God's character to her daughter-in-law as she witnessed his working on their behalf: 'He has not stopped showing his kindness to the living and the dead' (Ruth 2:20). Like all his attributes, it is one in which he is rich.

When we say God is rich in kindness, we declare that it is beyond our understanding and infinitely beyond any human display of kindness. As we catch glimpses of its vastness, we may be greatly moved by it. In his diary one morning, Andrew Bonar wrote, 'Last night I dreamed that I got such a view of God's kindness and benefits to me, that for some time my throat felt choked. I could find no way of giving utterance to my over-whelming feeling of wonder. When I awoke the savour of this still remained with me.'[1] God's kindness is never to be presumed upon, and it does not mean that he will not punish the guilty (Romans 2:4; 11:22). Rather, his kindness should lead us to repentance.

The most important manifestation

The greatest expression of God's kindness is his gift of salvation through our Lord Jesus Christ. Kindness is said to have 'appeared' when he entered the world (Titus 3:4). The word 'appeared' indicates that something happened with our Saviour's coming that had never occurred before. This unique event dramatically changed the course of human history. Truth about God became visible in a manner that was totally unexpected. It happened like a great light suddenly becoming visible. The Old Testament prophetic promise was that 'the sun of righteousness' would 'rise with healing in its wings' (Malachi 4:2). 'The rising sun' came 'to us from heaven to shine on those living in darkness and in the shadow of death, to guide our feet into the path of peace' (Luke 1:78-79). God entered our world in human form: 'The Word became flesh and made his dwelling among us.' Eyewitnesses declared: 'We have seen his glory, the glory of the One and Only, who came from the Father, full of grace and truth' (John 1:14). John's phrase 'full of grace and truth' parallels Paul's words 'the kindness and love of God our Saviour appeared' (Titus 3:4).

In the Lord Jesus' redeeming sacrifice on our behalf, God perfectly lays bare his love and kindness. It is breathtaking and overwhelming. God has not only saved us from the punishment of sin, but has also raised us up with Christ, and made us to sit with him in the heavenly places. In the ages to come, he is going to show the incomparable riches of his kindness towards us in Christ Jesus. Every Christian is an example and proof of God's amazing kindness.

The Lord Jesus both spoke of and revealed God's kindness. When he said, 'My yoke is easy' (Matthew 11:30), 'easy' is an adjective derived from the noun 'kindness' used in Galatians 5:22. It was used of a yoke that was well fitting. As a carpenter in Nazareth, oxen would have been brought to Jesus so that they could be measured for wooden yokes. Having taken the measurements, he would have roughed the yokes out before the oxen were brought back for them to be fitted properly. Then he would have checked each one carefully to ensure that it did not chafe the oxen's necks. There could well have been a sign outside the carpenter's shop, proclaiming, 'Our yokes fit well.'

Before new birth and discipleship of the Lord Jesus Christ, his demands may seem great, and even extreme. But the truth is that the burdens he puts upon us are never too much. To serve him is to prove his kindness. In the last sermon the evangelist D. L. Moody preached, he testified, 'I've worn God's yoke for over forty years, and I've always found it easy... There's nothing sweeter than to obey God's will. He is not a severe task-master.'

The definitive teaching

Significantly, Jesus' teaching on kindness, in what we commonly call the Sermon on the Mount (Luke 6:27-38), is the most detailed and practical in the Bible. It was only as he 'appeared' and made plain its reality that its full attractiveness could be described and defined. Every part of his teaching was illustrated by his own character and dealings with people.

Seven emphases

Luke 6:35-36 refer to God's kindness and mercy. The conduct our Saviour outlines is the reflection of God's character in us, once we have become his children through the new birth.

1. *Kindness means loving our enemies, and doing good to those who hate us* (Luke 6:27). While we were God's enemies, the

Lord Jesus Christ loved us and gave himself for us. We are to do the same.

John Brown exercised an influential ministry in eighteenth-century Haddington in East Lothian, Scotland. A minister in another branch of the church chose to speak of him with scathing language. Later on, this same minister was overtaken by misfortune. Because John Brown knew that he would not accept help from him, he sent it by other means so that the source was not known. When the man died, John Brown generously offered to take one of his destitute children, and bring him up with his own family. Although it turned out that the offer did not need to be taken up, it showed kindness, in doing good to those who had shown the opposite.

2. *Kindness requires us to bless those who curse us, and to pray for those who mistreat* us (Luke 6:28). When our Saviour's tormenters 'hurled their insults at him, he did not retaliate; when he suffered, he made no threats' (1 Peter 2:23). Instead, he prayed for their forgiveness.

3. *Kindness means that if someone hits us on one cheek, we let him hit the other one too; if someone takes our coat, then we let him have our shirt as well* (Luke 6:29). When the Lord Jesus was wrongly arrested, he instructed his disciples to reject violence, and he said nothing when soldiers gambled for his clothes at the foot of his cross.

4. *Kindness requires us to give to everyone who asks us for something, and if anyone takes what is ours, not asking for it back* (Luke 6:30). Beggars and others in need, many of whom would have been ignored because of their 'nuisance' factor, were always acknowledged by Jesus. He taught his disciples to listen to their requests and to care for their needs. This requirement, like the previous one, is not to be fulfilled with an

unthinking literalism. We are not meant to be 'a soft touch' since discernment is required as we respond to genuine need. But our Saviour's words are to be taken seriously and acted upon. It is better to be taken in by a fraudulent beggar than to pass by a person in genuine need.

5. *Kindness works by doing to others what we would want them to do for us* (Luke 6:31). Even if they have regarded themselves as our enemies by their actions we are to continue to do good to them, lending and expecting nothing back (Luke 6:32-36). While Jesus' enemies were conspicuous in their hatred and malice, he never retaliated. Instead, he expressed his concern for them.

6. *Kindness refrains from judging others* (Luke 6:37). Although the Lord Jesus Christ is the one whom God the Father has appointed to be the Judge of all, throughout his ministry he made plain that he had not come to condemn. Those whom others were presumptuous enough to condemn, he refused to censure. A sundial in Spain has an interesting and telling motto engraved upon it: 'I mark only the bright hours', a reminder to forget evils done to us and to remember only the good. One of F. W. Faber's hymns has the timely words, 'When we ourselves least kindly are we deem the world unkind. Dark hearts, in flowers where honey lies, only the poison find.'[2]

7. *Kindness is marked by generous giving* (Luke 6:38). The New Testament reveals 'the grace of our Lord Jesus Christ, that though he was rich, yet for [our] sakes he became poor, so that [we] through his poverty might become rich' (2 Corinthians 8:9). Explorers, trapped on frozen wastes near the South Pole, knew that their arrival at their base was in jeopardy. Their food supply dwindled to just a few biscuits in each of their knap-sacks. That night while they slept, their leader awoke as he

heard movement. He saw one of his companions stretch out his hand to the knapsack of the youngest member of their party. Fear gripped him. Had they sunk so low that they were stealing from one another? Happily, his fear disappeared, however, as he saw the man take half a biscuit out of his own bag and place it in the other member's knapsack. This older member had noticed that the youngster's strength was failing and that he was too proud to allow anyone to share his rations with him. So he had decided to act secretly. In the cold of an Antarctic night, an expression of love made their shelter warm with the glow of kindness.

Every day we may show kindness by our words. 'A very kind college president … framed a small sign and hung it on the wall leading to his office in the administration building on the campus. Only three words appeared, but they spoke with eloquence, inviting students and faculty into it: KINDNESS SPOKEN HERE.'[3] Proverbs 12:25 is a significant verse in this respect:

> An anxious heart weighs a man down,
>   but a kind word cheers him up.

Many languages have proverbs that similarly express the power of kind words. One from Japan asserts: 'One kind word can warm three winter months.' A Russian proverb declares: 'A word of kindness is better than a fat pie.'

The most telling example Jesus gave

A danger with familiar parts of the Bible is that we may take them for granted and neglect to look at them closely. The best example of human kindness is the Good Samaritan. The story and its context are important.

On one occasion an expert in the law stood up to test Jesus. 'Teacher,' he asked, 'what must I do to inherit eternal life?' 'What is written in the Law?' he replied. 'How do you read it?' He answered: '"Love the Lord your God with all your heart and with all your soul and with all your strength and with all your mind"; and, "Love your neighbour as yourself."' 'You have answered correctly,' Jesus replied. 'Do this and you will live.' But he wanted to justify himself, so he asked Jesus, 'And who is my neighbour?'

In reply Jesus said: 'A man was going down from Jerusalem to Jericho, when he fell into the hands of robbers. They stripped him of his clothes, beat him and went away, leaving him half-dead. A priest happened to be going down the same road, and when he saw the man, he passed by on the other side. So too, a Levite, when he came to the place and saw him, passed by on the other side. But a Samaritan, as he travelled, came where the man was; and when he saw him, he took pity on him. He went to him and bandaged his wounds, pouring on oil and wine. Then he put the man on his own donkey, brought him to an inn and took care of him. The next day he took out two silver coins and gave them to the innkeeper. "Look after him," he said, "and when I return, I will reimburse you for any extra expense you may have." Which of these three do you think was a neighbour to the man who fell into the hands of robbers?' The expert in the law replied, 'The one who had mercy on him.' Jesus told him, 'Go and do likewise'

(Luke 10:25-37).

The assumption is that the injured man was a Jew and Jews refused to have anything to do with Samaritans, a hostility with a long history. This gives all the more point to Jesus' choice of

the Samaritan as the individual who showed kindness to the
assaulted traveller.

The Samaritan exhibited love for someone who viewed him
as a hated enemy. He did to others what he would have wished
them to do for him in similar circumstances. He loved not only
the people who loved him, but also those who hated him.

Since Jesus gave this story as an example of what loving our
neighbour means, let us explore how it illustrates kindness as
love with its working clothes on.

Kindness is never taken by surprise

First, the Samaritan 'as he travelled, came where the man was;
and when he saw him, he took pity on him' (v. 33). Kindness
takes the unexpected in its stride. It is moved by people's need
when others may choose not to see it or to pass it by.

Kindness acts in practical ways

The Samaritan then 'went to him and bandaged his wounds,
pouring on oil and wine' (v. 34).

The South African politician Cecil Rhodes was about to enter
a room in evening dress for a meal when he noticed that at the
table at which he was to sit there was a young guest who was
informally dressed. He went back to his room and hastily
changed back from evening dress into his crumpled working
clothes in order that the young man might not be the only one
at his table informally dressed.

Kindness takes care of details

The Samaritan's oil soothed the injured man's wounds and the
wine cleansed them. The first-century Roman writer and

statesman Seneca wrote, 'People pay the doctor for his trouble; for his kindness they shall remain in his debt.' In the twentieth century an American similarly wrote, 'In the sick room, ten cents' worth of human understanding equals ten dollars' worth of medical science.'[4]

Kindness is prepared to put itself at risk in the service of others

The Samaritan put himself in some danger if those who had robbed the man were still in the vicinity. The Samaritan then 'put the man on his own donkey, brought him to an inn and took care of him' (v. 34). We can almost feel the care he took not to hurt the wounded man as he lifted him. We can guess too at the delay and inconvenience his kind actions caused him, but all such reasons or excuses were put aside in view of the attention his 'neighbour' required.

Kindness acts generously

The first thoughts of kindness are not 'How far dare I commit myself?' but rather 'What needs to be done at once?' 'The next day he took out two silver coins and gave them to the innkeeper. "Look after him," he said, "and when I return, I will reimburse you for any extra expense you may have"' (v. 35). His kindness was shown in generosity, and his generosity did not flinch at undeclared future demands.

Go and do the same!

Jesus' questioner was left in no doubt about how love expresses itself in kindness and pity. He was instructed, as are we: 'Go and do likewise' (v. 37).

To walk humbly

Kindness to others is a condition of pleasing God, and of walking humbly with him. He takes issue with us if it is absent from our life.

As Micah tellingly reminds us:

> He has showed you ... what is good.
>   And what does the LORD require of you?
> To act justly and to love mercy
>   and to walk humbly with your God
>
> (Micah 6:8).

To love mercy

Loving mercy and showing kindness go hand in hand with walking humbly with God. They affect and enhance our fellowship with him. D. L. Moody, the evangelist whom we mentioned earlier, regularly got up early to devote the first hour of the day to Bible reading and prayer. One morning as he sat down at his desk to study, he happened to look out of the window and saw a young fellow with a heavy case, walking towards the station three miles away. Not giving it much thought, he turned his eyes to his Bible, but try as he might, he could not fix his mind on what he was reading. He looked out of the window again. Something within him said, 'You ought to take that boy to the station.' He tried to persuade himself that it was not his duty. He made another effort to study, but it was no use. He jumped up and drove quickly until he reached the boy. He took him and his luggage and drove to the station. His comment as he arrived home is significant: 'I took up my Bible, and I didn't have the slightest trouble in fixing my mind on my work.'

To reveal God's character

Kindness is one of many evidences of new birth, for by it we reveal our heavenly Father's character. It is a characteristic of our new nature that is continually renewed as we learn more about our Saviour, who has created this nature within us. While powerfully showed in our actions, it is also seen in the way we look at people and speak to them.

The power of kindness

Kindness is potent in all relationships. Two neighbours were involved in a dispute. One sent a message to his neighbour, 'Never at any time set foot on my land.' The other responded: 'You are very welcome to walk on my land at any time, and even more to come and visit me in my home.' He won over his neighbour.

The most powerful influence in our coming to repentance and faith in our Lord Jesus Christ is our dawning awareness of God's kindness (Romans 2:4). Not surprisingly, therefore, God often chooses to use his kindness — reflected in his people's lives by his Spirit's fruit — to bring about the conversion of others. Souls are not won by harshness but by kindness. The apostle Peter understood this, and urged his readers: 'Live such good lives among the pagans that, though they accuse you of doing wrong, they may see your good deeds and glorify God on the day he visits us' (1 Peter 2:12).

Few Christians exercised greater influence in the fourth and fifth centuries than Augustine of Hippo (354-430). Someone who had a strategic place in his life and his conversion was Ambrose, the Bishop of Milan. Augustine does not explain how he came to meet Ambrose, but what he said is significant: 'I was brought by God to him in order that I should be brought by him to God.' He then went on to say, 'I came to love him, not at first as a teacher of truth, but for his kindness towards me.'[5]

The founder of the Penny Post, the beginnings of the British postal system, was Sir Rowland Hill. Returning home one evening, a man with a gun waylaid him and demanded whatever money he had on him. As Rowland Hill looked at his attacker, he could see that he was not a hardened criminal, and that he was highly agitated. He asked him how much he needed and why. His attacker, overcome with emotion at such questions, acknowledged that he had never done anything like this before, but that he was desperate to feed his starving family. Rowland Hill gave him what money he had, and promised him more if his attacker would call at his home. The man melted into tears. Rowland Hill instructed one of his employees to find out what he could about the man. The man's story was true. He lived in miserable housing and the first thing he did with the money was to buy bread for his family. His wife enquired whether he had obtained it by innocent means, and as he told her the story, they all cried for joy. Rowland Hill rehoused the man and his family and gave him employment. Such kindness was used to bring about the man's conversion, to the benefit of his whole family.

Kindness makes its own returns, as do so many aspects of the Spirit's fruit.

> Cast your bread upon the waters,
>> for after many days you will find it again
>>>>>> (Ecclesiastes 11:1).

Practical action

We do well to examine our own kindness to others in the light of the example of the Good Samaritan and the even greater example of our Lord Jesus Christ.

- Are our words and actions kind?
- We must begin with our hearts and thoughts.
- Our attitude is to be that of our Lord Jesus Christ.
- Ponder God's kindness.
- Then, as his spiritual children, let us go and do the same, in the power of his gracious Spirit!

7.

Goodness

Opinions about goodness vary. Some consider it scarce. 'Goodness is rare,' declares an old Latin proverb. Others even consider its pursuit dangerous. Pessimistically, Mark Twain wrote, 'Be good and you will be lonesome.'

Pictures and illustrations of virtues inevitably possess flaws but water is a useful one because of helpful similarities. Water, while essential to life, is often taken for granted. It is noticed by its absence more than its presence. It always seeks the lowest place. Likewise, goodness is never proud and does not draw attention to itself.

The goodness of God

An appropriate starting point is a Bible statement about God's character. 'You are good, and what you do is good' (Psalm 119:68). Aspects of God's character stand out because they show how completely different he is from us, marking him out as God. The apostle John, for example, highlights God's holiness and love when he writes, 'God is light' and 'God is love' (1 John 1:5; 4:8). If we had to choose one attribute of God above all others, we would not be far wrong if we chose his goodness.

When Moses wanted to see God's glory, God told him, 'I will cause all my goodness to pass in front of you, and I will proclaim my name, the LORD, in your presence' (Exodus 33:19).

When we affirm that God is good, we are declaring that he is all that he ought to be as God. His holiness and love — to which the apostle John draws our attention — are part of his goodness, as are all other aspects of his character. If we consider our own characters and lifestyle, one thing we may say without argument is that we are *not* all that we ought to be.

Since the Fall in the Garden of Eden, human goodness, at best, has been flawed. We have all sinned and fallen short of God's glorious standard of goodness (Romans 3:23). By nature, not one of us consistently does good; evil rather than good is the more natural fruit of our lives (Matthew 12:34). The more we know ourselves, the more we recognize that good does not naturally live in us. Even though we possess the desire to do good, we are often not able to do it. Instead of doing the good we want, we find ourselves doing wrong (Romans 7:18-19). Whether therefore we have in mind our being all that we ought to be as parents, children, employers, employees, citizens, friends and neighbours, we are deficient.

In creation

Not only *is* God good, but he also *does* good. Good works flow from his goodness. The first visible exhibition of this was at the beginning of all things, in the creation. As God created the light, the dry ground and the seas, the plants and the trees, the lights in the sky, every sort of fish, bird and animal and humankind, his goodness was declared (Genesis 1:4, 10, 12, 18, 21, 25, 31; cf. 1 Timothy 4:4).

God's creative works, displaying his goodness, are too numerous for us to comprehend. All the teeming creatures of the earth, sea and sky, both large and small, prove his goodness as he

provides food at the proper time for each so that they are satisfied. His unceasing renewal of the earth's resources similarly
sets forth his goodness (Psalm 104:24-30). Paul and Barnabas
gave testimony to the crowds at Lystra that God 'has not left
himself without testimony: he has shown kindness [literally, *doing
good*] by giving you rain from heaven and crops in their sea-
sons; he provides you with plenty of food and fills your hearts
with joy' (Acts 14:17; Psalm 85:12). God fills the hungry with
good things (Luke 1:53).

In his gifts

God's goodness is especially shown in his gifts and dealings
with Christian believers. Whatever is good and perfect comes
from him with unchanging consistency (James 1:17). There is
no limit to the good he bestows upon his children. Having given
us his Son, he graciously gives us everything else we need
(Romans 8:32), blessing us with every spiritual blessing in the
heavenly realms because we belong to our Lord Jesus Christ
(Ephesians 1:3). In his goodness, he gives us his good Spirit, as
the perfect Father who knows the best gifts his children need
(Nehemiah 9:20; Luke 11:13).

In his Word

All God's commandments and directions for human life are
good. To follow them is to be kept from disgrace (Psalm 119:39;
Romans 7:12). His Word is good, and the best food for our
souls (Hebrews 6:5). It is full of his good promises to us, and
not least in perfect salvation. Little wonder that God's message
in Jesus is uniquely *good* news (Romans 10:15) and when we
receive it his *good* work begins in us (Philippians 1:6). Essential
to that *good* news is the *good* hope he gives us in his Son for
the future (2 Thessalonians 2:16). It is a totally reliable hope

because its foundation is God's eternal faithfulness. Our experience of his unfailing promises is essential to our testimony of his goodness (1 Kings 8:56). It is a stimulus to our keen anticipation of what is yet promised in the future.

In his purposes

God's will and purposes for our lives are also good. He does not withhold any good thing from those who live their lives in obedience to him (Psalm 84:11; Romans 12:2). Even when he needs to discipline us, it is always for our good. David sadly went astray, disobeying God's Word. God chose to humble him in ways David does not define. But David's testimony was, 'It was good for me to be afflicted so that I might learn your decrees' (Psalm 119:67-71). 'Our fathers disciplined us for a little while as they thought best; but God disciplines us for our good, that we may share in his holiness' (Hebrews 12:10).

The conclusion is plain: God is good and what he does is good. His goodness may be put to the test in that we are encouraged to 'Taste and see that the LORD is good.' He is so good that he makes all who trust in him truly happy (Psalm 34:8).

The perfect model and example

Goodness finds its model and example in our Lord Jesus Christ for he is 'the image of the invisible God' (Colossians 1:15). His character and ministry, recorded in the four Gospels, display his unqualified goodness and its outflow in good works. Spontaneously people called him 'good' (Matthew 19:16; Mark 10:17; Luke 18:18). Nowhere was his goodness displayed more powerfully and movingly than in the manner in which he submitted to the humiliation and sufferings of the cross. He willingly endured the pain of unjust suffering in submission to his Father's sovereign will and purpose, and for our salvation, leaving us an example that we should follow in his steps (1 Peter 2:19-24).

David's testimony to God, 'You are good, and what you do is good,' was strikingly displayed in our Saviour's life. The apostle Peter preached for the first time to non-Jews when God brought him into contact with Cornelius and his household. In summarizing the life of the Lord Jesus, of which he had such personal knowledge, Peter said, 'God anointed Jesus of Nazareth with the Holy Spirit and power, and ... *he went around doing good'* (Acts 10:38). Those few words encapsulated the whole ministry of Jesus. He did good not sporadically but continually. No inconvenience, danger or opposition deterred him.

Our Saviour's earthly life and ministry serve to define and illustrate the goodness we are to emulate. He acted justly, loved mercy and walked humbly with God his Father. He practised full obedience to God's law, something he did also for us that he might be able to stand in our place as the law-breakers. He put aside his own well-being and comfort to achieve our highest good. He was our *Good* Samaritan. He delighted to give and did not look to receive. He focused on the needs that required to be met rather than the merits of those in need.

Goodness in us

The basic content of our lives as Christian believers is to be goodness and its active pursuit. That objective demands integrity so that what people see should be what we really are. In computer terms, the acronym WYSIWYG stands for *What you see is what you get.* It is a way of expressing that what we see on a computer screen is exactly what a printer will reproduce.

We indicated earlier that when we say that God is good we are declaring that he is all that he as God ought to be. New birth means we are born into God's family and are indwelt by his Holy Spirit. A new life is then present within us. Our characters, therefore, should reflect his, as should our actions. Although there is nothing wholly good in us as fallen human beings, all Christians, born again by God's Spirit, and made new people in Christ, begin to reflect their Creator and Redeemer's character in how they behave.

The word translated 'goodness' in the list of the fruit of the Spirit conveys the idea of moral excellence. Along with righteousness and truth, it is identified as the product of light (Ephesians 5:9). Brought into fellowship with God who is Light, the Holy Spirit prompts within us good ambitions and desires, together with the faith and power to achieve them (2 Thessalonians 1:11). We find ourselves wanting to reflect our Heavenly Father's character (Matthew 5:45; 3 John 4, 11), exhibited as it is in his Son. That is not without daily conflict with our old nature but we know where the victory must lie.

Transformation from bad practice and habits to those that are good becomes the order of every day (Ephesians 4:28). It is not an exaggeration to say that we should be 'full of goodness' (Romans 15:14), 'wise about what is good, and innocent about what is evil' (Romans 16:19). Goodness should be almost tangible.

The London *Daily Telegraph* recorded an interview with Lord Mackay of Clashfern when he was a member of the British Government. The journalist commented: 'Lord Mackay of Clashfern is still the great enigma of this Government. He is the oldest, cleverest and highest paid member of the Cabinet, a man of palpable goodness and unassailable moral authority, a man, moreover, whom *everyone* likes. And yet time after time he upsets the Tory rank and file with his difficult reforms.'

It is practical

Goodness is visibly practical in its outworking. As William Blake said, 'He who would do good to another must do it in minute particulars; general good is the plea of the scoundrel, hypocrite and flatterer.' Goodness does not leave until tomorrow the good it can do today. It encourages submission to civil authorities (1 Peter 2:13-17), employers (1 Peter 2:16-18), and to one another (Ephesians 5:21; 6:1-3; 1 Peter 3:1-6, 8). It causes us to respond with patience to opposition and suffering (1 Peter 2:20; 1 Peter 3:17), and does not allow anything to hinder us from pursuing what is right (1 Peter 3:6). It is God's chosen answer to unjust opposition to Christian witness (1 Peter 2:15-16; 3:1-6).

It results in good works

Goodness does not exist in a vacuum — it *does* things. While good works have no place in obtaining salvation (Ephesians 2:8-9; Titus 3:5), they are a principal evidence of the experience of it (James 2:17). We are born again to do good works God has prepared in advance for us to *do* (Ephesians 2:10). They are part of our true worship of God since they prompt people to praise our Heavenly Father (Matthew 5:16). They make the teaching about God our Saviour attractive in the eyes of the world (Titus 2:9-10). John Wesley appropriately urged his hearers: 'Do all the good you can, by all means that you can, to all the people that you can, for as long as you can.'[1]

Good works cannot be defined exhaustively since unique situations require unique solutions. Nevertheless, the principles and motivation behind them are plain. Goodness knows the importance of the tongue, and that speech cannot be separated from actions. It aims at speech that builds others up (Ephesians 4:29) and avoids speaking evil (Titus 3:1-2).

Goodness never pays back wrong for wrong but instead tries to be kind (1 Thessalonians 5:15), not only to fellow-Christians but to everyone (Galatians 6:10). It expresses itself in down-to-earth good deeds such as bringing up children well, showing hospitality, doing menial tasks, helping people in trouble, and being ready to do whatever is good whenever the opportunity presents itself (1 Timothy 5:10; Titus 3:1). It causes us to see that our regular income is intended to enable us to be rich in generosity (1 Timothy 6:17-18). Such activities are practical goodness. We are to be *glued* to what is good — that is the literally meaning of Romans 12:9: 'cling to what is good'.

An outstanding New Testament example

Our efforts so far show how difficult a quality goodness is to describe or define. It is best seen in its expression in people's lives. Interestingly, only two individuals in the New Testament — besides our Lord Jesus Christ — are described as good; and both, originally, had the name Joseph. The infrequent use of such a description is no doubt due to the recognition that no one can be justified before God through good works. The first, Joseph of Arimathea, went to Pilate after the crucifixion and asked for Jesus' body in order to provide a decent burial (Luke 23:50). The second is Barnabas, whose original name was Joseph, of whom we know much more. Barnabas' life illustrates how goodness is expressed in human life.

The source of Barnabas' goodness was plain: it was the fruit of the Spirit. He is described as 'a good man, full of the Holy Spirit and faith' (Acts 11:24). Neither he nor those who knew him well were in doubt as to the spring from which the goodness in his life flowed. As a believer, he was 'full of ... faith' — his life had the Lord Jesus Christ, 'the author and perfecter of our faith' (Hebrews 12:2), as its focal point. As a glorious benefit of faith in him, like all believers, Barnabas received the Holy Spirit who both began and continued God's good work in him. His goodness was an evidence of his spiritual union with the Lord Jesus.

A personal relationship with God

The description of Barnabas as good tells us something about his heart, and his personal relationship with God through our Lord Jesus Christ. Using the picture of a tree, the Lord Jesus explained: 'Every good tree bears good fruit, but a bad tree bears bad fruit. A good tree cannot bear bad fruit, and a bad tree cannot bear good fruit' (Matthew 7:17-18). He complemented this by saying later, 'The good man brings good things out of the good stored up in him, and the evil man brings evil things out of the evil stored up in him' (Matthew 12:35). Changing the picture from a tree to soil, Barnabas' heart proved to be good soil that yielded a plentiful crop (Luke 8:8).

Life in God's will

Barnabas' description also indicates that he lived in God's will, a will that is 'good, pleasing and perfect' (Romans 12:2). He proved that God's will is good and that it results in good. Living in God's will, he was not jealous of other people's gifts or resentful of 'playing second fiddle'. When he first entered into partnership with Paul, or Saul as he was also known, Luke, the author of Acts, writes of 'Barnabas and Saul' (Acts 11:30; 12:25; 13:2, 7); but then suddenly the order of the names switches and it is always 'Paul and Barnabas' (Acts 13:46, 50; 15:2, 22, 35). To begin with in the partnership, Barnabas, the older believer, naturally took the lead. But as Paul grew in grace, spiritual grace, understanding and gifts, he assumed the leading role. There is no indication that Barnabas ever resented this. He rejoiced to see the grace of God at work in other people's lives (Acts 11:23).

The description of Barnabas illustrates the power of goodness in at least four ways.

1. *It made him eminently trustworthy and reliable.* He was a man in whom the leaders of the early church had confidence and whose judgement could be trusted. For example, news had reached the early church's leadership in Jerusalem of a remarkable work of God's Spirit in Antioch. Christians had scattered after Stephen's death and the persecution that followed, and they 'gossiped' the gospel wherever they went. The leaders had no doubt about the choice of the best person to investigate and report to them — Barnabas (Acts 11:22). He could also be totally trusted with the stewardship of large sums of money. He, along with Paul, was given custody of the gifts of many Christians to help needy believers in Judea (Acts 11:30).

2. *The fruit of the Spirit in goodness prompted Barnabas to care for others.* It was Barnabas who brought Paul into the fellowship of the church at Jerusalem at a critical moment (Acts 9:26-28). When others treated Paul with coldness and perhaps suspicion, Barnabas gave him the warmth of genuine friendship and fellowship. No doubt Barnabas prayed for Paul thereafter and had his well-being and progress in the Christian faith on his heart. He was sensitive about how difficult it was for Paul to be accepted by some believers because of his reputation, before his conversion, as a persecutor of Christians. Assigned to work among Gentile believers in Antioch, Barnabas took the trouble to go to Tarsus to look for Paul and to bring him into partnership with him in his task (Acts 11:25-26). As we

consider Paul's subsequent contribution and influence in the church, we see how important that was.

Barnabas cared for others selflessly. Like Paul, he worked for a living in order to be able to give his services freely (1 Corinthians 9:6). Entitled to receive financial support from God's people, both chose not to do so out of motives of what we may here describe as goodness. They wanted neither to put a financial strain upon believers, nor to dishonour the gospel through any accusation that they were doing what they did only for the money.

3. *Barnabas' goodness put him in a position where he could exhort and encourage others with integrity.* Arriving at Antioch, he exhorted the believers to remain faithful to the Lord and to be steadfast in purpose with all their hearts (Acts 11:23). He could make such exhortations acceptably to other believers because what he taught and preached was conspicuously true in his own life. Through his life and testimony, others were brought to the Lord and other Christians encouraged.

All that we have discovered about Barnabas did not make him perfect for none can achieve that. He was not 'too good to be true'! Paul's letter to the Galatians records how Barnabas was sadly carried away by the unfortunate example of Peter and others at Antioch and played false to what he knew was true. Many Galatian believers were Gentiles, and together with Peter and others, Barnabas used to eat with them, something that Jews generally refused to do. But when James and other leading Jewish Christians from Jerusalem arrived to visit the Galatian believers, Peter 'began to draw back and separate himself from the Gentiles because he was afraid of those who belonged to the circumcision group. The other Jews joined him in his hypocrisy, so that by their hypocrisy *even Barnabas was led astray*' (Galatians 2:11-13). That little word 'even' is significant.

His action was completely out of character and reminds us never to forget that the best of people are vulnerable if they take their eyes away from the Lord Jesus and his example.

4. *The fruit of the Spirit in goodness was so evident in Barnabas' life as he encouraged others that the early Christians gave him his name!* He is first introduced in the book of Acts at a time when the early Christians were alleviating material needs by sharing possessions and property. Outstanding among them was 'Joseph, a Levite from Cyprus, whom the apostles called Barnabas (which means Son of Encouragement)' (Acts 4:36-37). His generous action was in sharp contrast to the actions of Ananias and Sapphira (5:1-11). While his name 'Barnabas' was more than a nickname, nicknames often speak volumes about a person's character, as this new name certainly did.

When I was a young Christian I remember hearing a sermon on Barnabas' change of name. The speaker explained how the name Joseph comes from a primitive root that means to add, or to do something again, and it is used sometimes to strike a negative note. The suggestion made was that when Barnabas was born he was one of a large family. In thinking of a name, his parents could only think of 'Another One', something not altogether complimentary! Others have felt the same. Lord Denning wrote, 'When I was born — two months earlier than expected — I nearly died. Mrs. Roe hurried across the road, wrapped me in blankets, gave me brandy — and I lived. She knew what a hard time my mother was having with the others all so young. She said as she wrapped me up, "That's one we could have done without."'[2] This could well have been why Barnabas' parents chose the name Joseph. Although we cannot be certain about the reason for the choice of name, we can be sure about his new name of Barnabas. The apostles called him Barnabas 'which means Son of Encouragement'.

The encouragement he gave to others was part of the Spirit's fruit of goodness in him.

No higher tribute could have been paid to Barnabas than this: 'He was a good man.' We can say with certainty — for it is the nature of goodness — that he was the person least aware of the goodness his life displayed. Those in whom goodness most grows are most aware of how little they have attained it.

We all have a reputation, although we probably do not know what it is. Some of us even have nicknames. God is glorified when either our reputation or our nickname indicates the attractiveness of the fruit of the Spirit in us. We cannot all be equally gifted, but we can all produce the fruit of the Spirit in goodness. We cannot all be physically beautiful or attractive, but we can all bear the fruit of goodness. We cannot all be great in terms of human greatness but, as a Greek proverb says, 'Goodness is not tied to greatness, but greatness to goodness.'

Do we have a nickname? Perhaps we do without knowing anything about it! How do we imagine others think of us? That is not an unimportant question since the Bible says, 'A good name is better than fine perfume' and 'more desirable than great riches' (Ecclesiastes 7:1; Proverbs 22:1). How would people describe us? Would they include the word 'good'? What value do we place upon goodness and good works?

Practical action

What then must we do to encourage this fruit?

• Deliberately think about goodness and things that are good. Paul urges the Philippians, 'Whatever is true, whatever is noble, whatever is right, whatever is pure, whatever is lovely, whatever is admirable — if anything is excellent or praise-worthy — think about such things' (Philippians 4:8).

- Fix our eyes upon our Lord Jesus Christ and consider his goodness.
- Give attention to discovering and doing the 'good works, which God prepared in advance for us to do' (Ephesians 2:10).
- Remember and be encouraged by an ordinary man who exemplified goodness.
- Pray that we may be like Barnabas!

8.

Faithfulness

Have you noticed how the study of the fruit of the Spirit becomes as much a consideration of God's character as of the character he wants us to exhibit?

When we think about it, that is what we would expect. The spiritual fruit we are considering is that of the Holy Spirit, the third person of the Trinity. He aims to reproduce in us our heavenly Father's character and our Saviour's likeness. It is appropriate that as we proceed we are compelled to exclaim, 'Lord, how wonderful you are!' That is certainly so as we now consider faithfulness.

Contemporary translations uniformly render the seventh aspect of the Spirit's fruit as faithfulness rather than faith. The same Greek word, *pistis*, is used for both, so it has to be translated and interpreted according to the context. Commonly used for faith and trust in God, here it is used in the sense of fidelity, the character of someone who can be relied on.

God's character

The New Testament, like the Old, often focuses upon God's faithfulness (e. g. 2 Thessalonians 3:3; 2 Corinthians 1:18;

2 Timothy 2:13; Hebrews 10:23; 11:11). This is understandable since his faithfulness is the solid foundation of our faith. How is it that we can put our faith in God with such confidence? It is because he is faithful.

The contemporary world provides few genuine certainties upon which we may depend. The sun, the moon and the stars, so vital to the maintenance of physical light to the universe, seem to be among the most constant things. Yet, they have their own changes, variations and shadows. God, who made them, is entirely different from them — he does not change. He is completely consistent (James 1:17).

He is absolutely reliable

God's character inspires total confidence because of his absolute reliability. His faithfulness is a consequence of his holiness (Isaiah 49:7) and is fundamental to our assurance of salvation in our Lord Jesus Christ. Self-contradiction is a moral impossibility for God (2 Timothy 2:13). Our confidence to live the Christian life depends upon this assurance. 'God, who has called you into fellowship with his Son Jesus Christ our Lord, is faithful,' Paul declares confidently to the Corinthians (1 Corinthians 1:9).

God's faithfulness is also essential to our confidence in his help when challenges and temptations come, for, as Paul affirms, 'No temptation has seized you except what is common to man. And God is faithful; he will not let you be tempted beyond what you can bear. But when you are tempted, he will also provide a way out so that you can stand up under it' (1 Corinthians 10:13).

The Old Testament particularly stresses God's faithfulness because the Jewish people knew, and know, themselves to be God's covenant people. Their men carry on their bodies the sign of that covenant — circumcision. Basic to his revelation to them was that he is the God who keeps 'his covenant of love to a thousand generations of those who love him and keep his commands' (Deuteronomy 7:9). As they entered the Promised Land after forty years of desert wandering, they proved God's faithfulness to his promises: 'So the LORD gave Israel all the land he had sworn to give their forefathers, and they took possession of it and settled there' (Joshua 21:43). Expressed in human terms, the Lord is the God who does not lie: he does not change his mind, and he never makes promises without fulfilling them, no matter how great or vast the time-scale — a truth relevant to both the first coming of our Saviour and the second (Numbers 23:19; cf. Titus 1:2).

Besides promising to order and direct all the events of our life for our greatest good, God guarantees to preserve, support, provide and deliver us. Once God has given his promise, no matter how distant in time the fulfilment may be, the promise may be regarded as already kept. Romans 8:30 expresses this truth in its use of the past tense 'glorified': 'And those he predestined, he also called; those he called, he also justified; those he justified, he also glorified.' So sure is our glorification in God's future purposes for us, it may be referred to in the past tense! William Grimshaw expressed this certainty of God's faithfulness quaintly but pointedly: 'Why, before the Lord will suffer His promises to fail, He will lay aside His divinity, He will un-God Himself.'[1]

He sustains his creation

God's faithfulness is not simply the experience of the Jews as a covenant people but also that of all his creatures since as the faithful Creator he sustains all he has made (Jeremiah 33:20). Since the flood in the days of Noah, the world has escaped God's judgement by water because of his promise not to repeat it, a guarantee expressed in the sign of the rainbow (Genesis 9:13).

God's faithfulness is described by the use of many meaning-ful adjectives.

1. It is *great* (Lamentations 3:23) in the sense that it is greater than any other and is totally sufficient.
2. It is *incomparable,* so that the question can be asked, with-out fear of contradiction,

> O LORD God Almighty, who is like you?
>> You are mighty, O LORD, and your faithfulness surrounds you
>
> (Psalm 89:8).

The latter thought expresses the infinity of God's faithfulness.
3. It is *immeasurable* in that it can be said to reach to the skies, and is past measurement as the skies are to us (Psalm 36:5).
4. It is *everlasting,* extending to all generations, beyond the possibility of betrayal (Psalm 89:33; 119:90).
5. It is *certain* for it is built upon sure foundations beyond the reach or power of any to attack or spoil (Psalm 89:2; Isaiah 54:10).
6. It is *unfailing,* even though our conduct and lack of faithful-ness deserve otherwise (2 Timothy 2:13). Our unfaithful-ness does not dilute his faithfulness.

Charles Spurgeon, the nineteenth-century Baptist preacher, recalled being received into church membership. 'I was much impressed, in my younger days, by hearing a minister, blind with age, speak at the communion table, and bear witness to us who had just joined the church, that it was well for us that we had come to put our trust in a faithful God; and as the good man, with great feebleness and yet with great eagerness, said to us that he had never regretted having given himself to Christ as a boy, I felt my heart leap within me with delight that I had such a God to be my God. His testimony was such as a younger man could not have borne: he might have spoken more fluently, but the weight of those eighty years at the back of it made the old man eloquent to my young heart. For twenty years he had not seen the light of the sun. His snow-white locks hung from his brow, and floated over his shoulders, and he stood up at the table of the Lord, and thus addressed us: "Brethren and sisters, I shall soon be taken from you; in a few more months, I shall gather up my feet in my bed, and sleep with my fathers. I have not the mind of the learned, nor the tongue of the eloquent; but I desire, before I go, to bear public testimony to my God. Fifty and six years have I served Him, and I have never once found Him unfaithful. I can say, 'Surely goodness and mercy have followed me all the days of life, and not one good thing hath failed of all that the Lord God has promised.'"[2]

Our Lord Jesus Christ

As with all God's attributes, they shine in glorious perfection in the life and character of our Lord Jesus Christ. Looking forward to the Messiah's coming, Isaiah promised:

Righteousness will be his belt
    and faithfulness the sash round his waist
                                                (Isaiah 11:5).

Nowhere is the accomplishment of that prophecy better expressed than in John 1:14: 'The Word became flesh and made his dwelling among us. We have seen his glory, the glory of the One and Only, who came from the Father, full of grace and truth.' When used of a person, truth has in view personal excellence, that candour of mind that is free from pretence, falsehood, and deceit; in other words, faithfulness. The same glory of God that Moses witnessed as the Lord passed in front of him — the glory of his graciousness and faithfulness — the disciples witnessed in the Lord Jesus.

The apostles, who spent the three most important years of their lives observing the life of Jesus and listening to his words, could never forget his faithfulness. At the Last Supper, knowing that all of them were going to forsake him, in spite of their protestations to the contrary, Jesus washed their feet, taught them and gave them wonderful promises. John's profound comment at this point in Jesus' ministry is: 'Having loved his own who were in the world, he now showed them the full extent of his love' or, as the Authorized Version puts it, 'he loved them unto the end' (John 13:1).

The disciples were left in no doubt about their Lord's faithfulness to them. It was the inevitable consequence of his love. His faithfulness assured them of their future reunion with him and their heavenly destination: 'In my Father's house are many rooms' (John 14:2). That promise was immediately followed by the words, 'If it were not so, I would have told you.' In other words, 'You know that you may utterly rely upon what I promise because I have proved myself faithful to you ever since you first followed me.'

John's later vision of the Lord Jesus Christ, in the glory of heaven, focuses significantly upon his faithfulness: 'I saw heaven standing open and there before me was a white horse, whose rider is called Faithful and True' (Revelation 19:11). This was an unspeakable comfort to the many persecuted and threatened Christians to whom the book of Revelation was first directed, just as it has been to succeeding generations.

Christian character

As a *good* tree consistently bears *good* fruit, so spiritually healthy Christians grow in faithfulness. Faithfulness does not happen accidentally. It arises from what we are, and the people we are becoming as a result of new birth. While peeling an onion may not be a good illustration from the point of view of its smell or the tears it brings, it is an excellent illustration of how faithfulness is not a matter of outward profession but of inner reality. What people see on our outside should be matched by every inner layer of our character being the same. Along with love, faithfulness should be deep within our heart, an important way of our showing how attractive the gospel of Christ is in transforming human lives, as it makes us trustworthy in everything (1 Timothy 3:11; Titus 2:10).

Faithfulness is a growing virtue, for as we are faithful in small matters so we will be found faithful in large ones (Luke 16:10). Much testing through trials may often be necessary to promote its progress and maturity (James 1:2-4). God permits difficulties, uses them, and overrules them, with that end in view (Romans 5:3-4). Faithfulness may be developed and proved often only through testing. It may be put to the test so that our faith is refined by what can best be described as 'fire', but, where genuine, it stands the test and brings credit to God (1 Peter 1:7).

Our relationship to God and his Son

Faithfulness cements human relationships. It is the principal expression of our love to others.

Faithfulness is to characterize our relationship to God. The God-given gift of faith in him through our Lord Jesus Christ prompts us to grow in our understanding of God's glorious nature and character. That knowledge, in turn, produces in us a desire to be faithful to him, since that is the appropriate response on our part to his faithfulness.

The world provides many competitors for our loyalty, not least the acquisition of money, possessions and the pull of human relationships, especially with those of the opposite sex. 'No

servant can serve two masters,' the Lord Jesus instructs us.
'Either he will hate the one and love the other, or he will be
devoted to the one and despise the other. You cannot serve
both God and Money' (Luke 16:13). Putting human relationships before our relationship to God is probably where most
spiritual casualties occur.

We are to serve God faithfully by keeping and upholding
the faith, recognizing it to be a trust (2 Timothy 4:7). Sometimes it may involve fighting hard for it since it is under constant attack (Jude 3). The history of the Christian Church, for
example, especially in the last hundred years in China, illustrates this. One pastor, Mr Wang Ming-tao, became the target
not only of the authorities in China but also of nominal Christians, particularly because of the magazine he published and in
which he himself wrote.

> I already knew that if in this present time I faithfully pro-
> claim the Word of God — rebuking the sins, the evils and
> the doctrine-destroying teachings in the corrupted, nom-
> inal church — I should surely meet the opposition and
> persecution which met Martin Luther... Under these con-
> ditions the one who faithfully preaches the Word of God
> cannot but expect to meet opposition from some leaders
> in the Church and from 'Christians' who are spiritually
> dead, in the form of malicious slander and abuse. I know
> that this will come to pass. I am prepared to meet it. I
> covet the courage and faithfulness of Martin Luther...
> We are ready to pay any price to preserve the Word of
> God and we are equally willing to sacrifice anything in
> order to preach the Word of God... Let us be prepared
> to be faithful to the Lord at any cost![3]

When grace has begun its work in us, care needs to be taken
to stay true to the Lord with all our hearts (Acts 11:23). Besides
its relevance to the temptations of everyday life, faithfulness is

an urgent necessity when persecution or hardships result from our allegiance to our Lord Jesus Christ (Matthew 24:4-26). When faithfulness is absent, God brings a charge against us (Hosea 4:1-2; 6:4-7; Matthew 25:21, 23; Revelation 2:10). A meaningful picture underlines this.

The relationship we have with our Lord Jesus Christ as his people is of a bride to a bridegroom (2 Corinthians 11:2). What our Heavenly Bridegroom looks for most of all in his bride is purity — the purity of faithfulness. His true people are described as 'the faithful in Christ Jesus' (Ephesians 1:1). Even as we delight in the well-tested faithfulness of friends, so God delights in our faithfulness to him and his Son. Our human frailty sadly causes us to let him down often but, thankfully, our lack of faithfulness does not nullify his, since in no way can he be false to himself (2 Timothy 2:13). One of many imperatives of the Christian life is to think about how God always keeps his word, since it can only result in us increasing our desire to be faithful to him (Hebrews 10:23).

Faithfulness in marriage

Faithfulness is a priority in four other areas of relationships, the first of which is marriage. We have a contemporary battle on our hands in upholding marriage and its sanctity. A popular entertainer, for example, has suggested 'that marriage vows should be renewed yearly, like dog licences, because the original format was devised when people lived far shorter lives'.[4]

Clearly and unambiguously, God requires faithfulness in marriage. There is a perfectly good reason why the words 'for better for worse' appear in most marriage services, since they sum up what the Bible teaches. J. B. Phillips was a patient in hospital, and was impressed by the helpfulness of a fellow patient, a milkman.

Little by little, I was told of his own private life. He was a milkman, a strenuous and demanding task then as now, and he had had a few years of happily married life. Then his wife began to deteriorate mentally. She was in no sense violently insane, but became more and more retarded until she was mentally no more than a ten-year old child. The husband would have to wake up before 4 a.m., arrange for his wife's breakfast and lunch and then quietly, for safety's sake, lock her into their house until his duties stopped early in the afternoon. He would then spend hours reading to her or playing childish games. Apparently someone in the ward had suggested to him that it would be better all round if she were put away in a place for the mentally retarded. He was a man who rarely spoke at all, but at this suggestion he is reported to have said, 'Look, she's my wife and I married her for better or for worse. This may be the worse but it's my job to look after her. That's all there is to say.'[5]

The Bible's directions about faithfulness in marriage tend to be directed particularly at husbands, although not exclusively so. Husbands and wives are instructed to find total physical and sexual satisfaction in one another, never sharing their unique relationship with anyone else. Nowhere is it put more plainly than in the book of Proverbs:

Drink water from your own cistern,
    running water from your own well.
Should your springs overflow in the streets,
    your streams of water in the public squares?
Let them be yours alone,
    never to be shared with strangers.
May your fountain be blessed,
    and may you rejoice in the wife of your youth.

A loving doe, a graceful deer —
    may her breasts satisfy you always,
    may you ever be captivated by her love.
Why be captivated, my son, by an adulteress?
    Why embrace the bosom of another man's wife?
                                            (5:15-20).

Husbands and wives will be helped in their faithfulness to one another as they remember how they first fell in love, and the commitment they then made to each other. It is what the writer of Proverbs tellingly calls rejoicing 'in the wife of your youth' (5:18).

Significantly, when the New Testament lists the qualifications for a Christian leadership that is above reproach, faithfulness in marriage is the first item on the list (1 Timothy 3:2, 12). Faithfulness in marriage begins with the thoughts or the mind. Marriage must be honoured in spirit as well as in fact.

Purity of heart

It takes effort to maintain purity of heart. Foolish jesting with sexual innuendoes — so characteristic of a fallen world — must be shunned. The Lord Jesus says, 'You have heard that it was said, "Do not commit adultery." But I tell you that anyone who looks at a woman lustfully has already committed adultery with her in his heart' (Matthew 5:27-28).

Titillation has infiltrated every aspect of the media, and much of contemporary fashion unhelpfully emphasizes sexuality. Faithfulness will influence what we allow ourselves to watch and how we dress. Faithful husbands love their wives as they love their own body, and behave towards them with care, treating them with respect and honour, striving to love them as Christ loves the church (Ephesians 5:23-33). Faithful wives, being completely trustworthy, bring their husbands 'good, not harm' throughout their married life (Proverbs 31:12), so that they are their husbands' pride and joy (12:4).

Mutual honesty

An important area of faithfulness in marriage is mutual honesty. General Gordon, who died in 1885 while trying to save Khartoum from fire and sword, never married. He wrote to a friend, who had announced his engagement:

> 'A man who is not married cannot know his faults; a man's wife is his faithful looking-glass; she will tell him his faults. Some men who have sisters may know themselves, but it is rare. Therefore I say to you (as I have said before), "Marry!" Till a man is married he is a selfish fellow, however he may wish not to be. Remember that by marrying you are no longer free for quixotic expeditions; you are bound to consider your better half; nothing is more selfish than a married man seeking adventures which his wife cannot partake in. To me, aged, and having gone through much trouble, it seems that to marry in this way is the best thing a man should do, and it is one which I recommend all my friends to do. You say, "Why do not you follow your own advice?" I reply, "Because I know myself sufficiently to know I could make no woman happy."'
>
> It was a favourite theme of Gordon. 'Yesterday I saw Miss Nightingale,' he wrote to a friend, 'and said, "You and me, Miss Nightingale, are at a disadvantage in the world, we are not married, we have no looking glasses to tell us our faults." Miss N. looked astonished, and thought it was a proposal. What I meant was that unmarried men and women have no one who cares enough about them to say the truth.'[6]

Parents and children

The second area is the relationship of parents and children. We might think it unnecessary to encourage parents to be faithful to their children but the Bible does not allow us to take it for granted. Faithful parents are careful in training their children, recognizing that the course of their children's future hinges upon the preparation they receive initially at home (Proverbs 22:6). This instruction cannot begin too early, especially in the encouragement of children to learn to obey (4:1-4). Faithful parents not only teach their children the way of wisdom but also lead them along straight paths (4:11), conferring upon them the life-long benefit of godly example (20:7).

The greatest and best legacy faithful parents can leave children is an example of practical godliness. They will take time and trouble to tell their children about God's dealings with his people in the past, and with themselves, recognizing that this is part of their responsibility for the generations that are to follow so that their children, in turn, may tell their children and so on (Psalm 78:5-6).

Faithful parents diligently discipline their children because they love them (Proverbs 13:24). When older children go astray, as they may do, no matter how good the instruction they may have received, parents must keep on loving them, and assure their wayward children that they do. The door is to be open always, with 'welcome' on the mat.

Children have a duty to be faithful to their parents. The commandment 'Honour your father and mother' (Exodus 20:12; Ephesians 6:2) is the first commandment to which a promise is attached: 'that it may go well with you and that you may enjoy long life on the earth' (Ephesians 6:3; cf. Deuteronomy 5:16). Faithful children listen to their parents and do not despise them when they are old (Proverbs 23:22). They remember that their parents gave them life and care. Faithful children do not regard their parents' property lightly, and avoid the snare of imagining that what is wrong outside the family is permissible within it (28:24). Faithful children appreciate that they have duties as well as rights: they are careful, therefore, in their treatment of their parents, and make necessary provision for them (19:26).

Employment

The third area is daily work, whether as an employer or an employee. Faithful employers do not withhold proper wages since they know that their own Employer is the Lord himself to whom they must ultimately answer for their actions (Ephesians 6:9; James 5:4). They are to be as conscientious and responsible towards those who serve them as they expect their employees to be in their work on their behalf.

As employees, we are to show that we can be fully trusted since it is in this way we may 'make the teaching about God our Saviour attractive' to the world (Titus 2:9-10). We should never be rude or insolent to our employers or careless in our handling of their property or interests. Stealing, including the smallest things, is out of the question. Our reliability should be such that our work does not need checking, especially in the handling of money (2 Kings 12:15). Faithful Christian employees work for their human employers as if it were for the Lord Jesus Christ himself (Ephesians 6:5-8), a work ethic that gives it both dignity and attractiveness.

Queen Elizabeth I appointed William Cecil as her Secretary of State. Her assessment of him was shrewd: 'This judgement I have of you: that you will not be corrupted with any manner of gifts, and that you will be faithful to the state, and that without respect of my private will you will give me that counsel that you think best.'

Christian fellowship

The fourth area is Christian fellowship, since God's declared purpose is that all Christians should live in church fellowship. Both in the physical realm and the spiritual, 'God sets the lonely in families' (Psalm 68:6; Acts 2:42-47; Galatians 6:10). We are to be faithful brothers and sisters to one another in God's family because of our common relationship to our Lord Jesus Christ (Colossians 1:2). We should be eager to always believe the best of people (1 Corinthians 13:7). Where wrong needs to be put right, we must be faithful in speaking the truth in love. 'Wounds from a friend can be trusted' (Proverbs 27:6), and speaking the truth in love enables us to help one another in our spiritual growth within the body of Christ (Ephesians 4:15, 25).

Loyalty to other believers

Faithfulness demands that we stand by one another (Hebrews 10:33). Things do not always run smoothly in church fellowship. Mistakes are made, but that is no reason for unfaithfulness or disloyalty. Even when we may not be well acquainted with other Christians God brings across our path, we are to be faithful in serving them in practical ways like hospitality (3 John 5-8). They should receive a higher standard of care and service than they would ever receive from unbelievers (1 Timothy 6:2). To be faithful to one another we must make time, and seize opportunities to meet, to encourage and help one another (Hebrews 10:25). More is often achieved in spontaneous and casual conversations than in planned and deliberate appointments to meet.

Support for our leaders

In the context of the Christian fellowship to which we belong, an important aspect of faithfulness is the support of our spiritual leaders. Spiritual leadership is God's necessary provision for his people, and we are to respect those who work hard among us, who are over us in the Lord and who admonish us. We are to hold them in the highest respect in love because of their work. Their tasks are made easier as we strive to live in peace with each other (1 Thessalonians 5:12-13). Faithfulness to them means that we obey them and submit to their authority, so that their work will be a joy as they watch over us as those who must one day give account to the Chief Shepherd of the flock (Hebrews 13:17). If their work becomes a burden, because of our failure to support them faithfully, we will be the losers.

A desired quality

There seems no end to the application of the priority of faithfulness. It is essential if we are to teach others the faith and equip them for future leadership so that the faith may be handed on to others in its purity and entirety (2 Timothy 2:2). If our responsibility is to communicate God's Word to others, we are to speak it faithfully, as in the sight of God (Jeremiah 23:28) and as sent by him (2 Corinthians 2:17). Faithfulness demands that we renounce all that is underhand or insincere (2 Corinthians 4:2), ensuring that we pass on God's Word accurately and faithfully, not leaving anything unsaid that God wants us to say (Joshua 11:15; Acts 20:27).

Whatever service we render to others, we are to provide it faithfully (3 John 5). We know the difference between doing something out of a sense of duty alone, and doing it with pleasure and care. The latter is to be the pattern of our service of others. The stewardship of money and possessions is no easy task, but faithfulness requires that we use them in the interests of our Saviour's kingdom (Luke 16:10-11), recognizing that all we own is a gift from him (1 Chronicles 29:14).

A point of significance

The word faithful is used to describe many outstanding Christians of the Bible, such as Abraham (Nehemiah 9:8; Galatians 3:9), Moses (Numbers 12:7), David (1 Samuel 22:14), Daniel (Daniel 6:4), Timothy (1 Corinthians 4:17), Tychicus (Ephesians 6:21; Colossians 4:7), Epaphras (Colossians 1:7), Onesimus (Colossians 4:9), Silas (1 Peter 5:12), and Antipas the martyr (Revelation 2:13). Each has something to teach us.

It is no surprise to discover that faithfulness has great importance in respect of rewards, which the Lord Jesus promises to give on his return. He knows the truth about our faithfulness, as no one else (Revelation 2:13). Equal gifts, if used with unequal faithfulness, will be unequally rewarded (Luke 19:12-27); and unequal gifts, used with equal faithfulness, will be equally rewarded (Matthew 25:14-30). The commendation of the Lord Jesus awaits all believers who keep the faith and are faithful in service (2 Timothy 4:7-8). Significantly, those described in the book of Revelation as being in the closest proximity to our Lord Jesus Christ are those who have proved themselves faithful (Revelation 17:14).

Kenneth MacRae (1912-1963), a Free Church of Scotland minister who concluded his ministry in Stornaway, addressed a conference of ministers.

I remember when I was a young divinity student being unexpectedly called upon to take the services in the congregation in which I used to worship as a small boy. It was also the church in which the great Dr. Kennedy has exercised his ministry. I felt overwhelmed at the thought throughout the day and after the evening service felt greatly troubled, depressed and downcast. The church officer, a worthy man named Alexander MacLean, locally known as Sandy Clunas, was waiting for me in the vestry. He was built on a large size... When I came into the vestry he just put his big arms round me and said, 'Never you mind, my boy. As Mr. Finlayson of Helmsdale used to say, it is not, "well done, good and successful servant" but "well done, good and faithful servant."' What is going to count at the end of the day is not success but faithfulness.[7]

Practical action

- As our love for God grows as we contemplate his love for us, so too our faithfulness grows as we ponder his. Therefore, let us deliberately ponder it!
- The Lord Jesus' faithfulness to his first disciples — in loving them to the end — is the same faithfulness he shows to us. If we are faithless, he remains faithful (2 Timothy 2:13).
- Let us be faithful to God as the heroes of the faith were. Let us be uncompromising in our faithfulness to one another, always esteeming loyalty highly.
- Let us not despise little things. 'A little thing,' Hudson Taylor said, 'is a little thing. But faithfulness in a little thing is a great thing.'[8] The Lord Jesus said, 'Whoever can be trusted with very little can also be trusted with much, and whoever is dishonest with very little will also be dishonest with much' (Luke 16:10).
- Let us aim at *present* faithfulness rather than thinking of it as something in the future. As a young man, James Fraser, who gave his life to working among the Lisu people of China, wrote,

> The Lord bids us work, watch and pray; but Satan suggests, wait until a good opportunity for working, watching and praying presents itself — and needless to say, this opportunity is always in the future... Since the things that

lie in our immediate path have been ordered of God, who shall say that one kind of work is more important and sacred than another? I believe it is no more necessary to be faithful (one says it reverently) in preaching the Gospel than in washing up dishes in the scullery. I am no more doing the Lord's work in giving the Word of God to the Chinese than you are, for example, in wrapping up a parcel to send to the tailor. It is not for us, in any case, to choose our work. And if God has chosen it for us, hadn't we better go straight ahead and do it, without waiting for anything greater, better or 'nobler'?[9]

An older Christian wrote to a younger,

Do not look forward much; be faithful today, as a man who may die before tomorrow. And if you should live, sinners are perishing all around you; and eight or nine years hence will be too late to speak to them... Our time is short, our work is important, our charge is awful, and our account must be soon given. Oh that it may be done with joy and not with grief!

The letter goes on to say that the writer is indifferent to what salary the young man achieves,

but that you may be enabled to prove yourself a good and faithful servant, and that the Lord may address you as such in the day of account. I pray earnestly for this, both for your sake and for the Lord's glory.[10]

Godly men and women have always taken faithfulness seriously. The issues are too serious for light-heartedness.

9.

Gentleness

Some words do not translate easily from one language to another. The Greek word *prautes*, rendered in the New International Version as 'gentleness' and in the Authorized Version as 'meekness', is such a word. Men are sometimes described as *macho* in the image they want to display. They deliberately behave and dress in an aggressively masculine manner. Similarly, some women may no longer want to be described as more gentle by nature than men.

Of all the aspects of the fruit of the Spirit, gentleness (or meekness) is the most difficult to grasp, and probably the least appreciated by the world at large. Neither word is adequate on its own to express what is in view. They have to be held together. Besides constituting the outflow of love, they are both features of humility.

Gentleness and meekness are not commonly admired qualities. In contemporary use, they carry a suggestion of spinelessness or weakness, which is the opposite of the true definition. If applied to men, they might be thought almost effeminate. We have, therefore, some work to do to establish the proper place for these terms in our thinking and objectives.

Definition starting points

As with all aspects of the fruit of the Spirit, gentleness is part of the outflow of love, and is in complete harmony with the other components. When it was necessary for Paul to rebuke and discipline the Corinthians, he asked them: 'What do you prefer? Shall I come to you with a whip, or in love and with a gentle spirit?' (1 Corinthians 4:21). The fact that Paul asked such a question revealed the great change God had brought about in his life at his new birth and conversion.

When we first meet Paul in the Acts of the Apostles, he stands watching and consenting to Stephen being stoned to death — a treatment more severe than the whip. When we next meet him, he travels on the Damascus Road 'breathing out murderous threats against the Lord's disciples' (Acts 9:1). But that was *not* his mood when he wrote to the Corinthians whose bad behaviour so disappointed him. As the Spirit's fruit grew in him, the *macho* Saul became the gentle and meek Paul.

The New Testament frequently links gentleness and meekness with humility (Matthew 11:29; Ephesians 4:2; Colossians 3:12-13). As gifts of the Spirit, they are a fruit of the wisdom given by God (James 3:13).

There is a natural tendency for us to rebel against authority and to be critical of the leadership of those who are older. While the temptation is always present for this to be carried over into church life, the Spirit's fruit brings this under control. Peter knew it was right to urge, 'Young men ... be submissive to those who are older. All of you, clothe yourselves with humility towards one another, because, "God opposes the proud but gives grace to the humble." Humble yourselves, therefore, under God's mighty hand, that he may lift you up in due time' (1 Peter 5:5-6).

It may be an oversimplification to say that meekness relates especially to our relationship to God, and gentleness has more to do with our relationship to others. Nevertheless, that suggestion provides a starting point that we can modify, as necessary, as we go along.

Meekness

Meekness expresses itself most in submission to God. Job stands out as an Old Testament example. Even though he did not understand what God was doing in his life, he worked hard at meek surrender to God's will. Having lost not only valuable possessions but also precious members of his family, with worse to follow, he responded:

> 'Naked I came from my mother's womb,
>   and naked I shall depart.
> The Lord gave and the Lord has taken away;
>   may the name of the Lord be praised'
>
> (Job 1:21).

But this hard discipline brought rich dividends he could never have imagined: 'The Lord blessed the latter part of Job's life more than the first' (42:12).

In repentance

What we soon discover, and realize more and more, is that we cannot live the Christian life without making mistakes. If we do not repent of them, or if we brush them aside as unimportant, they spoil our fellowship with God and our usefulness. We cannot live the Christian life as God intends without being in active fellowship with other believers, and under the spiritual direction of church leaders. God's discipline may well come to us through those 'over us' in the Lord. Acceptance of this discipline requires the humility that meekness teaches, a 'must' if we are to know God's blessing upon our life (1 Peter 5:6). Our mistakes and shortcomings may be forgiven, remedied and learnt from to our profit when we meekly submit to God in repentance (James 4:10; 1 John 1:5-10).

In teaching

Our submission to God may be proved and confirmed every time we read or listen to his Word. If we are meek, we listen to the teaching and preaching of God's Word with the active desire to obey, even if obedience requires the acceptance of rebuke and the need for our repentance (James 1:21).

> [The Lord] guides the humble in what is right
> and teaches them his way
>
> (Psalm 25:9).

Such obedience enhances our Christian character and the pleasure our lives give to God.

In trials

Meekness sometimes grows best in winter weather and bitter storms. When we do not understand what hard things in life are doing to us, God helps us to trust him and to proclaim his unfailing love. When everything in life goes well and we have all we want, it is easy to say, 'It is well with me.' When the opposite may be the case, meekness enables us to say still, 'It is well with me — and with my soul.'

A submissive spirit to God's sovereign will is no small part of our sanctification and the growth of meekness. General Booth, the founder of the Salvation Army, lost the sight of an eye. His remaining eye was operated on for cataract, without success.

His son Bramwell was commissioned by the family to tell him the bad news. As General Booth received the news, his first words were in the form of a question: 'I shall never see your face again?' Then 'after a moment, calmly, very calmly, the General said, "God must know best", and after a pause, "Bramwell, I have done what I could for God and the people with my eyes. Now I shall do what I can for God and the people without my eyes."'[1]

Puts God first

Meekness makes every effort to choose God's will before self-will. Even if submission requires us to become as the scum of the earth and the refuse of the world, it accepts obedience to God's will and strives to please him. Someone has described viewing life as a blank cheque, made payable to God, the amount and the time of cashing being left to the drawer.[2]

The Acts of the Apostles records the death of Stephen, probably the first Christian martyr, and certainly the earliest recorded. Cruelly treated and humiliated, he responded with submission and humility, as his Saviour had done when crucified. Committing his spirit to God, Stephen prayed for his persecutors (Acts 7:59-60). Meekness may cry out to God for help, but it reverently accepts whatever his answer may be. Meekness prompts us to counsel ourselves, 'Be still before the LORD, and wait patiently for him' (Psalm 37:7). It discovers the unique peace that submission to him brings, best likened to that of a child at rest and quietened in its mother's arms:

> My heart is not proud, O LORD,
>   my eyes are not haughty;
> I do not concern myself with great matters
>   or things too wonderful for me.
> But I have stilled and quietened my soul;

like a weaned child with its mother,
like a weaned child is my soul within me

(Psalm 131:1-2).

Meekness does not need to understand God's will; instead it rests in the knowledge of its perfection. Mary, the human mother of our Lord Jesus Christ, displayed meekness when told by the angel Gabriel of her unique pregnancy: 'I am the LORD's servant … May it be to me as you have said' (Luke 1:38).

Gentleness

If meekness has to do particularly with our relationship to God, gentleness relates especially to our human relationships. As we are humble before God, we learn to be gentle in our dealings with others. Gentleness is synonymous with courtesy towards everyone (Titus 3:2).

Does not discriminate

Human respect is notoriously given primarily and lavishly to the rich and the famous, and not to the poor and the ordinary. James describes how easily believers may slip into this snare (James 2:1-4). Suppose someone of human importance comes into the local church. Immediately the stewards pass the word around. One of them makes sure that he or she has a comfortable seat, with a good view of the pulpit and the OHP or Powerpoint. A message is sent to the church secretary and he carefully includes a welcome to those who are visiting, looking at the place where the 'important' visitor is sitting.

On the other hand, someone commonly described as a 'down and out' comes in, and the stewards steer him away from the most comfortable seats, and perhaps deliberately direct him to the overflow meeting. Christian gentleness, however, is to be undiscriminating and uniformly exercised, often much to the surprise of the recipients or beneficiaries (Titus 3:2). Its unassuming nature makes us approachable and unforbidding since people perceive that we want to help them, and be their servants for the sake of Christ (Philippians 2:5-8).

Calms potential conflict

Gentleness helps us to be a calming influence in circumstances that are confrontational and potentially explosive. Where gentleness is exercised, difficult subjects can be discussed without bad feeling. Imagine getting into a car on a cold winter's morning to find that the windscreen is completely frosted over. When you close the door, the inside of the windscreen also frosts up because of your warm breath. You try to remove it by scraping it away. As soon as you do so, it returns. The solution is not found in the friction of rubbing it away, but in turning on the warmth of the heater of the car! So it is in human relationships.

Necessary tasks like teaching others and exercising spiritual discipline can be carried out satisfactorily only where gentleness dominates. As godly teaching is given with gentleness, even those who oppose it may be brought to repentance, and erring or wayward Christians brought back into fellowship (Galatians 6:1; 2 Timothy 2:25).

The Old Testament draws special attention to the example of Moses. Numbers 12:3 explains that he 'was a very humble man, more humble [or gentle] than anyone else on the face of the earth'. In the face of undeserved criticism, Moses did not give way to rage but instead prayed and interceded for the offenders. Miriam and Aaron — and especially Miriam — spoke against Moses because of his Cushite wife, and were jealous of the Lord speaking particularly through him. God punished

Miriam with leprosy. Instead of saying, 'That serves you right, Miriam,' Moses prayed for her restoration, a prayer God graciously answered. In the list of the fruit of the Spirit, faithfulness immediately precedes meekness or gentleness. Significantly, God describes Moses as his faithful servant in the same context (Numbers 12:7).

The best example

Gentleness was a promised characteristic of the Messiah in the Old Testament prophecies. In one of the Servant Songs of Isaiah God declares:

> 'Here is my servant, whom I uphold,
>   my chosen one in whom I delight;
> I will put my Spirit on him
>   and he will bring justice to the nations.
> He will not shout or cry out,
>   or raise his voice in the streets.
> A bruised reed he will not break,
>   and a smouldering wick he will not snuff out.
> In faithfulness he will bring forth justice;
>   he will not falter or be discouraged
> till he establishes justice on earth.
>   In his law the islands will put their hope'
>   (Isaiah 42:1-4).

Four points are worthy of note in this description.

1. Gentleness is *an essential part of being a true servant of God* and of others. 'Here', God is saying, 'is the one who embodies true servanthood, the one in whom I can delight.'

2. Gentleness is *associated with God's Spirit* at work in us. 'I will put my Spirit on him.' The conduct of the servant indicates the Spirit's presence and anointing.
3. Gentleness is *unostentatious* and does not advertise itself. He does not shout or cry out.
4. Gentleness is *not aggressive*, nor threatening and considers no one beyond help. It does not bruise. It does not brush aside those who are hurting.

The prophet Zechariah also anticipated the Messiah's gentleness:

Rejoice greatly, O Daughter of Zion!
   Shout, Daughter of Jerusalem!
See, your king comes to you,
   righteous and having salvation,
   gentle and riding on a donkey,
   on a colt, the foal of a donkey

(Zechariah 9:9).

These words were appropriately recalled as Jesus entered Jerusalem on what we commonly call Palm Sunday (Matthew 21:5).

Submission to his Father's will

Our earlier suggestion that meekness relates especially to our relationship to God and gentleness to our relationship to others is confirmed by our Saviour's behaviour. Submission to his Father's will was fundamental to his meekness. The initiative in the plan of salvation belonged to God the Father. 'God so loved the world that he gave his one and only Son, that whoever believes in him shall not perish but have eternal life' (John 3:16). In obedient submission to the Father, the Lord Jesus said,

'Here I am — it is written about me in the scroll —
  I have come to do your will, O God'
                                              (Hebrews 10:7).

The spiritual food that sustained him throughout his earthly ministry was doing the will of the one who sent him, and finishing the work his Father gave him (John 4:34).

The Lord Jesus provided a perfect example of submission in the Garden of Gethsemane when, anticipating the crucifixion and its implications, he prayed, 'Not my will, but yours be done' (Luke 22:42). It was also shown in his submission to the wrongs inflicted upon him as he discharged his destiny as God's suffering Servant:

He was oppressed and afflicted,
  yet he did not open his mouth
                                              (Isaiah 53:7).

In his outstanding little book *The History of Redemption*, Jonathan Edwards draws attention to our Saviour's meekness.

Christ's meekness was his humble calmness of spirit under the provocations he met with. None ever met with so great provocations as he did. The greatness of provocation consists in two things: the degree of opposition by which the provocation is given; and in the degree of the unreasonableness of that provocation, or in its being not only without reason, but likewise against the greatest degree of obligation to the contrary. Now, if we consider both these things, no man ever met with a thousandth part of the provocation that Christ met with from men: and yet how meek was he under all! How composed and quiet his spirit! How far from being ruffled or in a tumult! When he was reviled, he reviled not again; and 'as a sheep before her shearers is dumb, so he opened not his mouth.' No appearance was there of a revengeful spirit: on the contrary, what a spirit of forgiveness did he exhibit![3]

When insults were hurled at the Son of God, he said nothing back. Instead, he responded by entrusting himself to him who judges justly (1 Peter 2:23).

Concern for others

The second important aspect of the Lord Jesus Christ's gentleness or meekness was his thoughtful concern for others, as Isaiah predicted (Isaiah 42:2-3). Knowing, for example, everything about a Samaritan woman's disreputable past, he gently probed her conscience to bring her to faith and forgiveness (John 4:18). When others would have stoned a woman taken in adultery, although not excusing her sin or allowing her to continue in it, he treated her with courtesy and compassion (John 8:11). Zacchaeus, a corrupt tax-collector, could hardly believe his ears when he realized that Jesus knew not only his name but everything about him, and was still willing to enter his home as his guest and friend (Luke 19:1-10).

Jesus' disciples benefited from his considerateness in numerous practical ways. He was thoughtful towards them when they were tired (Mark 6:31), troubled and distressed (John 14:1-3). He included gentleness in his description of himself when he issued this invitation: 'Come to me, all you who are weary and burdened, and I will give you rest. Take my yoke upon you and learn from me, for I am gentle and humble in heart, and you will find rest for your souls' (Matthew 11:28-29).

Gentleness is such an important part of his character that we may rightly appeal to one another by it, as Paul did to the Corinthians when he wrote, 'By the meekness and gentleness of Christ, I appeal to you' (2 Corinthians 10:1). Paul wanted to plead with them, as he knew the Lord himself would do. It is interesting that Paul uses the two words we have employed to convey the Greek word *prautes*, and here the New International Version uses 'meekness' to translate it. Significantly, he 'appeals' to them and 'begs' them, rather than commanding them, even though he had authority to do so. Those words, and the attitudes they reflect, belong to meekness and gentleness.

Attempting a definition

We are now in a better position to attempt a definition of gentleness and meekness. **Gentleness, or meekness, is an inward attitude that enables us to be submissive to God's will, irrespective of difficulty, and to treat others with gentleness, humility, courtesy and care.** Aristotle, an expert in defining Greek words, defined meekness as the happy medium between excessive anger and excessive angerlessness. (As we think this through, we see how much self-control — the next and final aspect of the Spirit's fruit — fits in here.)

Submits to God

Meekness is synonymous with quiet submission to God and his commands and principles. In its expression towards other human beings, meekness means not responding violently when injustice or hurt are suffered, but instead reacting with care and sensitivity so as not to aggravate the difficulties. As someone put it centuries ago, 'Meekness takes injuries like pills, not chewing, but swallowing them down.'[4] Meekness aims at maintaining peace when we are bombarded with words, attitudes and actions calculated to provoke us.

Puts others first

When we are meek, we do not stand on our dignity or parade our rights. Genesis 13 describes how Lot moved about with Abram, his uncle, and they both had flocks and herds. The land could not support them while they stayed together, and quarrelling arose between the two groups of herdsmen. Abram took the initiative and said to Lot, 'Let's not have any quarrelling between you and me, or between your herdsmen and mine, for we are brothers. Is not the whole land before you? Let's part company. If you go to the left, I'll go to the right; if you go to the right, I'll go to the left.' Lot looked up and saw that the whole plain of the Jordan was well watered, so he chose that area for himself. The two men parted company, and Lot set out towards the east. By rights, Abram, the older man, should have had first choice. Meekly, he gave that choice to Lot, and when Lot chose selfishly, Abram chose to say nothing. But as soon as Lot left, God came to Abram and gave him the promise of tremendous blessing: 'Lift up your eyes from where you are and look north and south, east and west. All the land that you see I will give to you and your offspring for ever. I will make your offspring like the dust of the earth, so that if anyone could count the dust, then your offspring could be counted. Go, walk through the length and breadth of the land, for I am giving it to you' (vv. 14-17). God's instruction to Abram was a wonderful commendation of his meekness and an illustration of the blessing promised to the meek that they 'will inherit the earth' (Psalm 37:11; Matthew 5:5).

Practises forgiveness

Meekness practises the forgiveness our Lord Jesus encouraged Peter to adopt if his brother kept on sinning against him. 'Lord, how many times shall I forgive my brother when he sins against me?' Peter asked. 'Up to seven times?' The Lord Jesus answered, 'I tell you, not seven times, but seventy-seven times' (Matthew 18:21-22), and proceeded to relate a telling story about forgiveness. Meekness is the predisposition to be merciful and compassionate in dealing with the faults of others. It is the spirit in which we are to try to restore a fellow-Christian who falls into sin (Galatians 6:1).

The beauty of meekness and gentleness

The beauty of meekness and gentleness is in their practice. They are an essential part of the attractively distinctive clothing Christians are to wear daily (Colossians 3:12). As different groups or types of people are recognized by their uniform, so Christians should stand out for their gentle spirit and meek behaviour.

If we hear the words 'The Salvation Army', we probably think of a distinctive uniform and of people who serve the needy. The same may be said of nurses and other vocations. Similarly, without gentleness and meekness in our lives, we would be just as indistinguishable as they are without their uniform (Colossians 3:12; Titus 3:2). Whatever our natural temperament, these qualities are to be present, since they are essential to our calling. We are to pursue them with the enthusiasm of athletes running in a race (1 Timothy 6:11).

When people might expect us to be angry, meekness responds with restraint and courtesy, disarming our critics. When it is our duty to correct others, meekness does so without arrogance, impatience or irritation, bending over backwards to be faithful without unnecessary offence.

Pride and humility think differently. Pride is apt to think badly of others, but humility leads us to think ill of ourselves instead. Oliver Cromwell appropriately appealed to the General

Assembly of the Church of Scotland in the seventeenth century:
'I beseech you, in the bowels of Christ, think it possible you may
be mistaken.'[5] Meek Christians regard the example of the Lord
Jesus as the only acceptable norm for obedience to God and
the service of others (2 Corinthians 10:1; Philippians 2:5-8).

When window dressers want to display the attractiveness of
what it is their task to present, they carefully choose a background that will show off their product at its best. We too can
see how wonderfully attractive are the attributes of meekness
and gentleness when we measure them against the opposite
and unpleasant features of human behaviour like pride,
arrogance, jealousy, quarrelsomeness, resentment, abrasiveness,
anger, violence, aggressiveness and insensitivity.

Meekness obeys the instruction of Romans 12:14-21:

> Bless those who persecute you; bless and do not curse.
> Rejoice with those who rejoice; mourn with those who
> mourn. Live in harmony with one another. Do not be
> proud, but be willing to associate with people of low
> position. Do not be conceited. Do not repay anyone evil
> for evil. Be careful to do what is right in the eyes of every-
> body. If it is possible, as far as it depends on you, live at
> peace with everyone. Do not take revenge, my friends,
> but leave room for God's wrath, for it is written: 'It is
> mine to avenge; I will repay,' says the Lord. On the
> contrary:
>
>> 'If your enemy is hungry, feed him;
>>   if he is thirsty, give him something to drink.
>> In doing this, you will heap burning coals on his
>>   head.'
>
> Do not be overcome by evil, but overcome evil with good.

In the top nine

We are accustomed to listings and ratings, whether of sports men and women, football teams, universities, schools, best-selling books or recordings. In the Sermon on the Mount, the Lord Jesus Christ gives God's ratings concerning virtues, and meekness comes in the top nine (Matthew 5:1-11). Significantly, it comes after being 'poor in spirit' and 'mourning our sinfulness' (Matthew 5:5). It flows naturally from a true view of ourselves, and influences our relationships with others, especially in the respect we give to them. It is the opposite of self-assertion, and selling ourselves.

I was reading a presentation one of my granddaughters had to give in applying for university entrance. She is a modest girl with Christian convictions. As I read the draft it sounded self-assertive and even proud. I questioned her about it. 'Well,' she said, 'they say at school that we are just to sell ourselves and draw attention to our strengths.' As we talked together, we concluded that it was more important for her to be true to herself.

Be wary of pride

The more we know ourselves, the meeker we become since we realize the folly of having too high an opinion of ourselves. William Carey was invited to a dinner party at the home of the governor of India. When a guest asked a servant whether Carey had not once been a shoemaker, Carey, who had overheard what was asked, stepped forward and said, 'No, not even shoemaker, sir, just a cobbler.' Those who are genuinely humble are always sensitive to and wary of their pride.

John Wesley said, 'It is difficult to be humble. Even if you aim at humility, there is no guarantee that when you have attained the state you will not be proud of the feat.' The darling sin of Satan is 'pride that apes humility'.[6] Meek Christians recognize that they must measure the genuineness of their Christian profession by growth in humility.

Only through the new birth

The point must be made that true meekness is possible and achievable only by the Christian, and solely through the experience of new birth. Others may imagine that they can achieve it by other means, as, for instance, by Karate. The spirit of our age encourages unconditional self-regard rather than admission of sinfulness. The New Age movement encourages people not to find a Saviour outside of themselves but one within through realizing their own potential.

The spirit of independence and self-sufficiency is so rooted in our hearts as sinners, we may know ourselves as sinners only as God the Holy Spirit enlightens us. The more we know God the more aware we become of our sin. The more conscious we become of our sin, and repent of it, the meeker we become. The meekness and gentleness we have in focus are not the consequence of our genes but entirely the fruit of our new birth.

New birth and the spiritual life it gave was the explanation of Paul's growth in meekness, although he was almost certainly unaware of it in three statements he made in a telling time order.

1 Corinthians 15:9: 'For I am *the least of the apostles* and do not even deserve to be called an apostle, because I persecuted the church of God.'

Ephesians 3:8: 'Although I am *less than the least of all God's people*, this grace was given me: to preach to the Gentiles the unsearchable riches of Christ.'

1 Timothy 1:16: 'But for that very reason I was shown mercy so that in me, *the worst of sinners*, Christ Jesus might display his unlimited patience as an example for those who would believe on him and receive eternal life.'

From being 'the least of the apostles' to 'the worst of sinners' Paul revealed spiritual growth in meekness.

It was also evident in the life of David Livingstone. His biographer records: 'Sympathetic students of the Last Journals cannot fail to be impressed with the growth in him during those long years of depression and loneliness of a spirit of humility and charity. Meekness was not a virtue that by any stretch of imagination could be applied to the Livingstone of Kolobeng or the Zambezi, but this, too, begins from now on to take its place. A consciousness of his own failings is often evident, and from it there grows something deeper — a gentleness that comes very near to saintliness.' One of his friends wrote, 'Though his unflinching courage and determination remain where they ever were, his gentleness seems to have become more and more diffused through all he did.'[7]

Received with God's blessing

Meekness is identified in the Bible as a condition of receiving God's blessing (Psalm 37:11; Matthew 5:5). God makes gentleness and meekness to prosper because he delights in them (Psalm 149:4). While it may be a mystery and paradox to the unbelieving world, they are a secret of happiness, which is why they find their place in the Beatitudes.

The Greek word was used of tamed animals. Think of a young horse upon whose back no one has ever sat. It needs to be brought under control before it can be regarded as meek or gentle, and then useful. The same is true of a dog to be employed as a guide dog for the blind. It has to be taught to come to heel at a single word of command, and to act appropriately, whatever it encounters. There is much within us that similarly needs to be tamed — whether impetuous anger or impatience. 'Meekness is the bridle of anger,' the saying goes. Meekness and gentleness are not to be equated with weakness or spinelessness but rather with controlled strength, so that like a horse, our lives are brought under control, and like a guide dog, our lives serve and benefit others. Instead of being a display of weakness, they reveal strength. A college principal, a physical giant of a man, was outstanding for his gentleness and humility. His students called him 'the gentle giant' — a delightful tribute.

Meekness has power

A Turkish proverb urges, 'If someone hits you with a stone, hit him back with a piece of cotton.' John Brown of Haddington was influential as a pastor and teacher. The fruit of the Spirit began to grow in him while he was a young man. Belonging to a poor family, he helped an elderly shepherd called John Ogilvie in the mountains of Abernethy, in what is now Tayside in Scotland. On John Ogilvie's farm another young man worked, Henry Ferney, who delighted to tease and test John's Christian profession. One Sunday evening Henry thought he would provoke John Brown to anger. He hurried his own sheep to the fold, and then strewed the entrance, on which an open gate hung, with whins (prickly shrubs), and stacked a bunch of rough prickly ones near the post where the gate was fastened, knowing John Brown would soon come along with bare feet. This he did. 'He made his way bare-footed through the gorse, with sharp twinges of pain and barred the gate. As he withdrew, Ferney watched his opportunity, and sent him headlong with a

roar of boyish laughter. Young Brown rose with face, hands
and legs bleeding. Henry expected that at last he would now
hear an enraged tongue, or be summoned to fight. But he was
more than astonished when the victim of his crude joke looked
at him, and asked in a kindly but injured tone' why he had
done such a thing on a Sunday, and something John would
not have done to Henry. 'Henry was stung by the meekness of
his comrade, and was distressed till he was frankly forgiven.
From that hour, Henry Ferney became a staunch and steadfast
friend.'[8]

Practical action

What then of our meekness and gentleness? What in our life needs
to be brought under control to make us meek and gentle?

- Meekness, gentleness and humility cannot be achieved unless
  we examine ourselves, no matter how painful that may prove.
- We must confess everything within us that militates against
  meekness and gentleness, and most of all our pride. As Charles
  Wesley's hymn puts it,

> When I survey the wondrous Cross,
> On which the Prince of Glory died,
> My richest gain I count but loss
> And pour contempt on all my pride.

  Then we must carefully consider our Saviour's example so that
  'the mind of Christ' in us is encouraged.
- Then let us cry to God for the help of his Spirit to achieve daily
  the fruit of the Spirit in meekness.

On his way to Georgia in 1737 George Whitefield, the outstanding evangelist and preacher, prayed, 'God, give me a deep humility, a well-guided zeal, a burning love and a single eye, and then let men or devils do their worst!' He recorded five years later in his diary: 'I spent most part of my time in secret prayer... Pray that I may be very little in my own eyes, and not rob my dear Master of any part of his glory.'[9]

Cyril Forster Garbett, while Archbishop of York, drew up some special resolutions. The third was: 'To pray for humility: to turn any apparent slight or passing-over into an offering to God.'[10]

10.
Self-control

'Get a grip upon yourself' is not an uncommon comment. The Greek word for self-control in the New Testament comes from the word *strength* and means *to take hold of* or *to grip*. We see how necessary is the principle of self-control when we consider other words we associate with self — *self*-pity, *self*-importance, *self*-interest, *self*-centredness, *self*-deception, and *self*-deceit. Self is one of the toughest weeds that grows in the garden of our lives.

Two key New Testament passages about Christian leadership call for self-control as an essential qualification for holding office in the church (1 Timothy 3:2; Titus 1:8). Our Lord Jesus Christ calls us to self-control as part of the freedom bought for us at such tremendous cost by his atoning death. 'So if the Son sets you free, you will be free indeed' (John 8:36). Paul wrote, 'It is for freedom that Christ has set us free. Stand firm, then, and do not let yourselves be burdened again by a yoke of slavery... You, my brothers, were called to be free. But do not use your freedom to indulge the sinful nature; rather, serve one another in love' (Galatians 5:1, 13).

Self-control is, however, one of the most difficult aspects of the Spirit's fruit to achieve. The proof is the number of times we have to confess to God the same sins — some on a daily basis — because our best resolutions fail. Since it is 'the fruit *of the Spirit*', it is through him alone that we can attain it. The paradox is that we achieve it only as we are controlled by him.

As we reflect upon our past experience, we see that it is essentially our sinful desires that break our resolves to be self-controlled. As we are obedient to the Holy Spirit in the pursuit of holiness, we experience his power to withstand temptation and to walk instead in the way of Christ. Our essential weakness, however, always remains. Until the end of our human life we remain 'jars of clay to show that this all-surpassing power is from God and not from us' (2 Corinthians 4:7). Yesterday's victories over sin and temptation do not ensure victory for today. Thankfully, our weakness is no obstacle to God's power but he requires us to recognize our weakness and live accordingly. We must never lose sight of our need for absolute dependence upon the Spirit.

If self-control is absent, Satan finds us an easy target. Its absence makes us unhelpful to others and dishonouring to our Saviour. We shall all be judged with regard to our exercise of self-control.

Self-control as the climax of the Spirit's fruit

If love is the living spring from which all other aspects of the fruit of the Spirit flow, self-control is an essential element in the fruit's development.

- *Love*, while extravagant and lavish, does not spoil, since it is thoughtful love.
- *Joy*, though unspeakable, is not a joy expressed in a way that is insensitive to the sorrows and heartaches of others. Joy is not to be confused with exuberance that leads to excess.

- *Peaceableness*, so attractive when it is exercised, knows that there are limits beyond which the desire for peace cannot go.
- *Patience* can be exercised only through self-control. It continually puts reins upon impatience.
- *Kindness* is not blind to considerations that sometimes make it necessary to appear to be cruel in order to be kind. Generosity of spirit must not be unthinking, but under control.
- *Goodness* cannot have limits set upon it, but self-control enables it to exercise itself in the best interests of those who are to benefit from it.
- Both *faithfulness* and *gentleness* have to withstand many challenging tests, but self-control strives after their maintenance whatever the conflicting pressures.

The whole of life and everyone's life

While some virtues and qualities may be particularly appropriate at different stages of human development, self-control is relevant to all age groups and every stage of life (Titus 2:2, 5-6, 12). In Titus 1, when speaking of the self-control required of Christian leaders, Paul uses the same word as in Galatians 5. But in chapter 2 the word translated 'self-control' in the NIV is the word 'sober-minded'. The words go together helpfully in so far as we exercise self-control only as we are sober-minded or sensible about our way of life.

Titus 2:1-12 is a key passage in pointing to the universal need for self-control, and it merits pondering:

You must teach what is in accord with sound doctrine. Teach the older men to be temperate, worthy of respect, self-controlled, and sound in faith, in love and in endurance. Likewise, teach the older women to be reverent in

the way they live, not to be slanderers or addicted to
much wine, but to teach what is good. Then they can
train the younger women to love their husbands and children, to be self-controlled and pure, to be busy at home,
to be kind, and to be subject to their husbands, so that
no one will malign the word of God. Similarly, encourage the young men to be self-controlled. In everything
set them an example by doing what is good. In your teaching show integrity, seriousness and soundness of speech
that cannot be condemned, so that those who oppose
you may be ashamed because they have nothing bad to
say about us. Teach slaves to be subject to their masters
in everything, to try to please them, not to talk back to
them, and not to steal from them, but to show that they
can be fully trusted, so that in every way they will make
the teaching about God our Saviour attractive. For the
grace of God that brings salvation has appeared to all
men. It teaches us to say 'No' to ungodliness and worldly
passions, and to live self-controlled, upright and godly
lives in this present age...

Eating and drinking

The first application of self-control is to activities as basic as
eating and drinking, especially in a world in which restaurants
become temples of indulgence, cookery books a kind of liturgy,
and celebrity chefs are popular idols. Food and drink are among
God's everyday gifts, but that does not mean that they can be
enjoyed without care and thought. Benjamin Franklin, the
eighteenth-century American author, inventor and diplomat,
described how as a young man he was careful to control what
he both ate and drank. He found it beneficial in his studying,
and he wrote, 'I made the greater progress, from that clearness

of head and quicker apprehension which generally attend temperance in eating and drinking.'[1] Later in life, making a list of virtues, he put temperance at the top of his list of thirteen, with this comment: 'TEMPERANCE — Eat not to dullness; drink not to elevation'.[2]

There is a difference between *eating in order to live* and *living in order to eat*. The first is essential to life whereas the second is the path to gluttony. Too much food may not only lead to obesity but to ill health and a failure in our duty to treat our body as the temple of God's Spirit.

Contemporary society tends to regard social eating and the drinking of alcohol as inseparable, and that is nothing new. The Bible indicates that we should eat, not as an excuse for drunkenness but for strength (Ecclesiastes 10:17). Some choose not to drink alcohol at all, mindful that the issue is not simply whether it is good for them but if it is good for others who may follow their example and not be able to achieve moderation. No one would wish to be responsible for prompting future alcoholics to take their first drink. If we believe that social drinking has its place, self-control is vital because alcohol has the potential of producing the opposite.

Part of practical self-control may be to avoid keeping company with those who eat or drink too much (Proverbs 23:20). Self-control requires moderation:

If you find honey, eat just enough —
   too much of it, and you will vomit

(Proverbs 25:16).

Sex and purity

Lack of sexual self-control becomes lust. The seriousness of this aspect of self-control is underlined by how frequently it causes someone's downfall. This was certainly the case for God's wisest man, Solomon; God's strongest man, Samson; and God's most upright man, David.

Self-control keeps love pure and chaste. Our sexual appetites are God-given and necessary for the continuance of the human race. But God intends that they should be fulfilled only in marriage: 'At the beginning of creation God "made them male and female". For this reason a man will leave his father and mother and be united to his wife…' (Mark 10:6-7).

Nowhere will Christians stand out more in their family, work and community than in their recognition that to please God they must obey the instructions he gives about controlling their bodies in a way that gives them dignity and does not abuse them. Our sanctification, God's call to be pure, requires that we avoid sexual promiscuity (1 Thessalonians 4:1-8).

The mind is of crucial importance. We seldom, if ever, do anything without first thinking about it, whether deliberately or not. While television, videos, films, newspapers and books can, as most things, be used for good, they also have tremendous potential for sowing base thoughts and motives in our minds. Sexual self-control begins not with the use of our bodies and our sexual organs but with the thoughts we allow to enter our mind, particularly through the eyes. Does not most temptation come to us through what we see?

Even in marriage, sexual intercourse — a precious benefit of that unique relationship — is to be enjoyed in a manner consistent with self-control since Satan aims to spoil the gift (1 Corinthians 7:1-6).

Realism requires that we recognize the importance of self-control in social drinking and the control of sexual appetites. Because sexual appetites are so strong, the first thing that usually disappears when people drink too much is control of sexual desires. In December 2000 the British Government announced that from the beginning of 2001 the morning-after pill would be available from local pharmacists. A radio commentator suggested that it was disappointing that its issue was not in time for Christmas office parties.

Much of fashion, and especially women's, is calculated to titillate. *The Scotsman* newspaper printed an extract by Colin McDowall from the biography of Jean Paul Gaultier, the flamboyant couturier, significantly entitled *Dress for Excess*. Self-control avoids excess. It is appropriate to dress to be attractive and pleasing. But is it ever right to dress to arouse?

A caution

Focus upon sexual desires alone is a mistake, since self-control needs to be exercised over all desires that are at the expense of our soul: 'Dear friends,' implores Peter, 'I urge you, as aliens and strangers in the world, to abstain from sinful desires, which war against your soul' (1 Peter 2:11). While sexual desires are a problem, they are by no means the only desires with which we have to wrestle.

The straightforward test

Will this interest, activity, relationship — or whatever else is in view — be for the benefit or detriment of my life, and of my soul? Others may not appreciate the decision at which we arrive, especially if we once exercised no restraint (1 Peter 4:4), but our desire is not to please our contemporaries but God.

Honesty will lead us to conclude that the wisest course is often to avoid situations where we know we are likely to be tempted. All temptations, however, cannot be anticipated, since Satan will always throw new ones at us. Then wisdom will frequently dictate that we simply flee from them (2 Timothy 2:22), and then reflect on how best to be prepared for the next time.

Self-control in personal aspects of life

Let us briefly consider four areas.

1. *Our view of ourselves*

Self-control is necessary regarding the estimate we have of ourselves, so that we control our pride. If we are successful or admired, it is difficult not to think too highly of ourselves and not to believe the good things people may say about us. Behind public expressions of humility, conceitedness may hide.

When we take time to be truthful with ourselves and ponder our past record, basic weaknesses of temperament stand out. Only pride suggests that we do not have them. Self-control helps us to guard deliberately against giving in to them. For example, women know how susceptible men may be to a pretty face, although men may be loath to admit it. Self-control puts up its warning signs. Timothy, for example, appears to have been timid in temperament. Nevertheless, God called him to spiritual leadership. Paul instructed him therefore to fan into flame his God-given gift, and to remind himself that God has not given us 'a spirit of timidity, but a spirit of power, of love and of self-discipline' (2 Timothy 1:7).

2. *The need for self-control in speech*

Since our tongues may do more hurt than even our actions, the use of the tongue is to be a priority when applying self-control. James pointedly puts it like this: 'We all stumble in many ways. If anyone is never at fault in what he says, he is a perfect man, able to keep his whole body in check' (James 3:2). Only fools show their annoyance at once (Proverbs 12:16). Anger is easily expressed, but self-control stops us from allowing it to lead us into sin and disastrous consequences (Ephesians 4:26). Self-control is imperative if our tongue is to avoid being too quick to express criticism or to make rash promises (Ecclesiastes 5:2).

3. *Its relevance to our use of time*

Time is probably the most precious commodity we possess. Self-control is lacking when time is wasted or abused. The wisdom of Ecclesiastes 3:1-8 is beyond dispute:

> There is a time for everything,
> and a season for every activity under heaven:
> a time to be born and a time to die,
> a time to plant and a time to uproot,
> a time to kill and a time to heal,
> a time to tear down and a time to build,
> a time to weep and a time to laugh,
> a time to mourn and a time to dance,
> a time to scatter stones and a time to gather them,
> a time to embrace and a time to refrain,
> a time to search and a time to give up,
> a time to keep and a time to throw away,
> a time to tear and a time to mend,
> a time to be silent and a time to speak,
> a time to love and a time to hate,
> a time for war and a time for peace.

Sir John Laing proved the wisdom of this as a young man when he worked in his father's building business. His biography records that 'During this time he gave up rock-climbing. He felt that it was not right to take such risks, a fatal accident would leave his father to bear alone the increasing burdens and difficulties. The sacrifice of a favourite relaxation added to his need for self-discipline. He would sometimes go up to the rocks and look at them longingly, then turn away and satisfy himself with a walk on the fells.'[3]

The wisdom concerning the use of time taught in the book of Ecclesiastes requires self-control so that we make the most of every day and the opportunities it provides (Ephesians 5:15-16). If some of us are inclined to be lazy and slack in our employment of time, others may be the opposite and try to cram too much into every day to the detriment of quality of life and relationships. If we are among the latter, it is salutary to ponder that 'hurry is a form of violence done to time'.[4] Self-control helps us avoid the abuse of time.

If we never discipline ourselves to give space for relaxation, we may make mistakes and sin through the vulnerability exhaustion produces. It was when Elijah was exhausted that he was most susceptible to temptation (1 Kings 18 and 19). 'Though I am always in haste,' John Wesley wrote, 'I am never in a hurry; because I never undertake any more work than I can do thoroughly with perfect calmness of spirit.'[5]

4. *The place we give to money and possessions*

Covetousness is a deadly form of idolatry and we know constant pressures to live with a wholly materialistic outlook. We imbibe it from birth and acquisitiveness is widely endorsed as a legitimate goal, whether through wise investment or by gambling in the hope of winning a lottery. Contentment is seldom commended, and even less exhibited.

Paul Hodder-Williams was head of the publishing house, Hodder and Stoughton. In a Christmas message to his employees he wrote, 'I am heavily addicted to Mammon and only love God sometimes. All the really bad decisions I have made in life derived from a total underestimate of the spiritual values involved. Our enemy is materialism. And materialism is a preference for material possessions and physical comfort above spiritual values. We breath it in, we see it and feel it and hear it all day and every day. We become addicted to it.'

Self-control is imperative if we are to avoid the temptation and trap of wanting to get rich and thus wandering from the faith and plunging ourselves into spiritual ruin. The achievement of self-control in this area is assisted as we remind ourselves of three salutary truths.

- We can seldom add selfishly to our possessions without some- one else suffering.
- We brought nothing into the world, and we can take nothing out of it (1 Timothy 6:6-10).
- The best storage place for treasures is in heaven, and where our treasure is, our heart will be too (Matthew 6:19-21).

Subtle temptations accompany many of God's best gifts since Satan targets them to spoil them. Part of his evil strategy is to make a bad thing out of something that is good. The Corinthian Christians, for example, succumbed to the temptation of allowing their exercise of spiritual gifts to become selfish. They used them not for the edifying of the whole body of Christ but for personal 'ego trips' and selfish indulgence.

Self-control determines that whatever our spiritual gifts, they will not be employed to advertise our abilities or bolster our pride, but rather to assist and serve others. Then our philosophy will not be, 'Since God has given me this gift I ought to *enjoy* exercising it.' Instead, we will ask, 'Is there any way — large or small — that I can *serve* the body of Christ with this gift? What wise restrictions should I put upon its use so that everything is done in a fitting and orderly way?' (1 Corinthians 14:12, 26-33, 40).

An admirable quality

People and nations throughout the centuries have admired self-control.

The book of Proverbs declares:

Better ... a man who controls his temper than one who
  takes a city

                                                    (16:32).

I count him braver who overcomes his desires than him
who conquers his enemies, for the hardest victory is the
victory over self

                                                  (Aristotle).

He is most powerful who has power over himself

                                                   (Seneca).

He conquers who conquers himself

                        (Latin Proverb, *Vincit qui se vincit*).

No man is such a conqueror as the man who has de-
feated himself

                                       (Henry Ward Beecher).

The apostle Paul knew it was right to urge upon Timothy the priority of self-control. He used three pictures of people whose lives have to be marked by it if they are to succeed: the soldier, the athlete and the farmer (2 Timothy 2:1-7). The athlete is perhaps the most obvious. When we see an athlete on the winner's podium receiving a medal we recognize that we are acknowledging not only achievement, but also the self-discipline that brought it about. Behind all athletes who succeed in representing their countries are habits of self-discipline in getting the required hours of sleep, eating and drinking in moderation, and maintaining a generally disciplined lifestyle. Although it may sometimes cut them off from legitimate social activities they enjoy, none would criticize them for their self-denial since in no other way will they reach their goal. So it is in the Christian life.

Even the most undisciplined person admits a sneaking admiration for self-control since its attractiveness in others is real.

- *Purity* is more appealing than impurity.
- *Unspoiled married love and relationships* are more attractive than adultery and family break-ups.
- *Contentment* is more pleasing than selfish covetousness.
- *Love* is a more agreeable life-controlling factor than selfish ambition.
- *Control of one's feelings* is more constructive than outbursts of rage.

What is required?

The self-control required is self-mastery: 'Do not offer the parts of your body to sin, as instruments of wickedness, but rather offer yourselves to God, as those who have been brought from death to life; and offer the parts of your body to him as instruments of righteousness. For sin shall not be your master, because you are not under law, but under grace' (Romans 6:13-14).

As we follow the directions God gives, with the help of his Holy Spirit, we are not under the power or dominion of any sin or habit, but we *willingly* use our Christian freedom to serve the Lord Jesus Christ by serving others. The word 'willingly' is important since the change that comes into our lives is the consequence of God's grace in salvation through his Son. God's grace at work in us transforms our attitudes. 'It teaches us to say "No" to ungodliness and worldly passions, and to live self-controlled, upright and godly lives in this present age' (Titus 2:12).

Like many young men of my generation, soon after the Second World War, I had to do National Service for eighteen months. Although I did not remain with my training regiment, I spent the first weeks with the King's Royal Rifles, a regiment well known for its speed and quickness in marching. Those first weeks of basic training taught me things that have remained with me. When I was in Northern Ireland for a week to preach, I went out one morning to phone my wife. I noticed two young girls looking at me, but took no notice. As I came out of the phone box, one of them approached me and asked: 'Were you in the army?' 'Yes,' I replied. 'I thought so,' she said, turning to her companion. 'You walk just like my father.' Now that was some forty years after I had left the army! But the army *taught* me things that I have not forgotten. Grace does the same — it *teaches* self-control.

We may summarize what Paul says,

- as towards ourselves, self-control;
- towards the world, uprightness;
- and towards God, godliness (Titus 2:12).

Augustine expressed self-control in similar terms: 'To my fellow men a heart of love, to my God a heart of flame, to myself a heart of steel.' Paul's summary of the consequences of God's grace in our lives firmly underlines the priority of self-control. Neither uprightness in the world nor godliness towards God are achievable without it.

Self-control is essential to our conformity to the likeness of our Lord Jesus Christ (Romans 8:29). His whole life was disciplined to fulfil his Father's will (Luke 9:51; John 4:34). Behind all he did, there lay the secret discipline of prayer, a secret the disciples soon discerned and began to covet (Mark 1:35; Luke 11:1). His self-discipline helped him to withstand temptation (John 6:15) and to refuse to respond as the world might have expected in the face of ill-treatment (1 Peter 2:23).

The nitty-gritty of achievement

How may we help ourselves to achieve self-control? It will not be done without hard work. The illustration of the athlete underlines that truth. One of the most popular preachers of the fourth century was John Chrysostom, and he did not underestimate the difficulty of achieving self-control.

> The younger athletes practise on the bodies of their comrades the attack that one day they will have to launch on their opponents. Let this be a challenge to you. Practise yourself in the disciplines of true religion. You see many Christians unable to resist the paroxysms of anger, and others set on fire by the flames of lust. Practise resistance against such passions.[6]

Helpful principles and imperatives

1. *We must recognize that self-control is God's will.* Nothing God calls us to is impossible. Satan may whisper, 'It cannot be done!' He is a liar!

2. *We must put away excuses for failures.* Our sin is not so much in our failures but in our not picking ourselves up again and then, through God's forgiving grace and strength, trying again.

3. Remembering that the fruit is that of the Holy Spirit, *we must seek to be filled by him*, and avoid grieving or quenching him. The secret of self-control is the Lord Jesus setting up his government in our soul as we walk in obedience to his Spirit.

4. *We must make sure that our body is our servant and not our master* (1 Corinthians 9:27). That is relevant to eating and drinking, sexual appetites, and every other use of our body and its energies.

5. *It requires honesty and sometimes drastic action with regard to known sources of temptation.* It was in this respect that the Lord Jesus spoke about cutting off the offending members of our body — the hand, the eye, and the foot (Matthew 5:30; 18:8). He does not suggest literal self-mutilation but the recognition that our sinfulness is expressed in our use of these parts of our body, and that these are the areas where we are to do battle for purity.

- *Honesty is imperative.* There is no point in locking the front door if we leave a back door ajar. Self-control may demand the deliberate avoidance of situations or friendships, and sometimes the 'surgery' of cutting ourselves off from them, because of our vulnerability.
- *Honesty requires self-examination.* As athletes analyse their performance so that they learn from their mistakes, so we should do the same, not introspectively but with the positive desire to improve. Inevitably and rightly, self-examination will drive us to the cross to seek renewed forgiveness.

  Writing in his diary, after self-examination, Andrew Bonar put it like this: 'My heart sinks within me. I can only once again put my hand upon the head of the slain Lamb, and look up.'[7] 'This sent me this evening in all haste to hide myself in Christ.'[8] Appropriate action must follow self-examination, otherwise it may become unhelpful and even dangerous.

6. *Be specific in appropriate targets for self-control,* trying not to be too ambitious but realistic. We may achieve self-control in areas of life only as we are willing to name sin or temptation.

Paul Brand, later to become a famous surgeon, lived at home when he began work as a building apprentice. Early on, he had to learn self-control in the practical matter of getting up in the morning, without being dependent upon the help of his sister Connie.

In order to get to work at seven-thirty, an hour's ride across London by train, he had to get up at five-thirty. It wasn't easy. Connie, feeling keenly responsible, would herself rise at five, then come into his room and shake him every five minutes. Still he found it almost impossible to waken. 'This isn't right,' he finally decided. 'It's my problem. Let me solve it.' He purchased a huge two-bell alarm clock and set it beside his bed on a tin tray. It was Connie who had to turn it off. He slept through its tintinnabulations like a baby. 'It's because you don't really want to get up,' a helpful friend told him. 'Even when asleep you know what you're doing, and anything you really want to do you can do.' That night he set the alarm and ordered Connie not to wake him up under any circumstances. The second it started to ring he jumped up. The next night he reduced the amount of winding, and kept reducing it. He removed the tin tray. Then he removed one bell, after that the second bell, so the alarm went off with a mere rattling sound. Finally he wound it and turned it off, finding he could waken at the sound of its click. It was one of the most triumphant moments of his young life. He had proved he could master something.[9]

Setting aside a page for each day of the month in my prayer diary, I find it helpful to record aspects of my life where I need to exercise special care, such as pride and my giving. As I pray about them the Holy Spirit increases sensitivity at my stepping out of line and prompts me to ask for his unfailing strength.

7. *Adopt the positive attitude of the athlete* (1 Corinthians 9:24-27). Do not be tempted to feel sorry for yourself because of the discipline you have to exercise. Rather be grateful that you recognize it is necessary and know the benefits it brings. Once, this would not have mattered to you, but grace has set you free to be the person God wants you to be. What is more, the benefits extend beyond this life.

8. *Do not expect quick results but anticipate progress*. In Peter's telling list of virtues that he urges us to add to our faith, self-control is preceded by knowledge, suggesting that what we learn needs to be put into practice. It is significantly followed by perseverance: 'Make every effort to add to your faith goodness; and to goodness, knowledge; and to knowledge, self-control; and to self-control, perseverance; and to perseverance, godliness' (2 Peter 1:5-6). As Alexander Whyte put it, perseverance means 'falling down and getting up, falling down and getting up, all the way to heaven'.

Practical action

Our target influences the discipline we accept. If self-control seems a tall order, it is not when we recognize our aim — to please our Saviour. 'So we make it our goal to please him, whether we are at home in the body or away from it' (2 Corinthians 5:9).

The legendary snooker and billiards player, Joe Davis, was a guest on the BBC Radio programme *Desert Island Discs*. He 'claimed that he took such care of the suppleness of his hands that he wouldn't even drive a car before a match'.[10] If he was prepared to exercise such self-control for a human, transitory prize, how much better to be self-controlled for the eternal prize of pleasing our Saviour!

11.

Postscript

A beauty and benefit of the description of spiritual growth in terms of fruit is the potent reminder that fruit is not produced at once but always takes time to grow and mature. That principle has special application to our characters.

Fruit needs time to mature

The best fruit ripens naturally

We referred earlier to Charles Simeon. He was a contemporary of Henry Venn (1724-1797) who was more than thirty years his senior.

> Simeon, when he first made the acquaintance of the Venns, was still immature and needed a great many awkward corners knocked off his somewhat affected personality. This was so much the case that Henry Venn's daughter Eling, who was twenty-four at the time, never forgot her first impressions: 'It is impossible to conceive anything more ridiculous than his look and manner were. His grimaces were beyond anything you can imagine.

So, as soon as we were gone, we all got together into the study and set up an amazing laugh.' For this she and her two sisters were duly reprimanded. They were taken by their father into the garden and told to bring him a peach. But as it was still early summer they had to make do with an unripe one. 'Well, it's green now,' said the kindly old man, 'and we must wait; but a little more sun and a few more showers, and the peach will be ripe and sweet. So it is with Mr. Simeon.'[1]

Since fruit often takes a long time to mature the picture points to what should be the beauty of the fruit of the Spirit in old age. The writer of Psalm 92 uses a lovely picture to describe the righteous; that is to say, those in a right relationship with God.

> The righteous will flourish like a palm tree,
>   they will grow like a cedar of Lebanon;
> planted in the house of the LORD,
>   they will flourish in the courts of our God.
> They will still bear fruit in old age,
>   they will stay fresh and green,
> proclaiming, 'The LORD is upright;
>   he is my Rock, and there is no wickedness in him'
>   (Psalm 92:12-15).

The palm tree conveys the idea of gracefulness and the cedar is a picture of strength. Both gracefulness and strength find their source in their presence in the house of the Lord — another way of expressing fellowship with God.

As we get older, active physical functions in the body of Christ may be denied us, but our contribution by means of our characters and spiritual influence may continue, and even increase. While our bodies decay, our souls may do the opposite.

We are not to covet perpetual physical youth, like Peter Pan, but instead keep spiritually fresh without sterility, always giving testimony to God, our Rock.

Old age brings particular opportunities

The unique trials of old age provide special opportunity for increased fruitfulness of character. For most of us as we get older, our health deteriorates. We will be tempted to be self-pitying, pessimistic, frustrated and irritable. God's grace at work in us will encourage us to be thankful, optimistic on account of our living hope, contented and accepting of our circumstances.

As we get older, we need to lay down responsibilities, especially in leadership and service, so that others who are younger may exercise their gifts and abilities as we have. The temptation is then present for us to be critical of our successors and the succeeding generations, ever referring to 'the good old days'. But the fruit of the Spirit will cause us to love our successors and the rising generation, and to encourage them in every possible way.

The best fruit in our lives may be at the end! Our lives may be 'for the praise of his glory' (Ephesians 1:12) as much at their end as earlier, and even more so. It is a challenge to remember that the older we grow, the more we grow like ourselves. If we look at a crooked branch on a tree, it is salutary to remember that it is the result of years of crookedness.

Our fruit affects the life of the church

The fruit any of us bear, whether young or old, contributes health to the body of Christ. We influence one another, and most of all by character and behaviour. Children grow up like their parents, taking after them not only in looks but also in mannerisms and ways of doing things. It is uncanny sometimes to recognize this in children. Young Christians all too readily reflect the character of the older Christians with whom they fellowship and serve. Unconsciously we 'feed' off one another, as we are spurred on — or, sadly, sometimes, not spurred on — to love and good deeds (Hebrews 10:24).

Captain Cook, the eighteenth-century British explorer, records how the inhabitants of one place where his ship *The Adventure* stopped in the South Seas came out to them, as they were about to depart. 'Many canoes accompanied us out to sea with coconuts, and other fruits; and did not leave us till they had disposed of their cargoes. The fruits we got here greatly contributed toward the recovery of the *Adventure's* sick people. Many of them who had been so ill as not to be able to move without assistance, were, in this short time, so far recovered, that they could walk about of themselves.'[2] Many ills in our lives would find their cure if we helped one another more by the production of the Spirit's fruit in our character. As the fruit of the Spirit marks our conduct towards one another, we unconsciously nourish one another's spiritual health and well-being. It always encourages and refreshes.

The fruit is for God

The supreme motivation for the production of the Spirit's fruit in our lives is that it is for God's pleasure (Romans 7:4) — hence our title, *Living for God's pleasure*. He is the Gardener, and the fruit is produced for his satisfaction. The production of fruit is intended for his enjoyment and praise. As a gardener enjoys walking in his garden to see evidences of growth and beauty, so God looks in the garden he has planted — his church — for evidences of Christlikeness in those whom he has redeemed at such tremendous cost. The fruit that makes Christians both attractive and good advertisements of the gospel's power reflects God's own perfect being and character.

The fruit reveals the fulness of Christ in us

A distinction has to be made between the attributes of God that can be communicated to us and those that cannot. God does not impart his almighty power or supreme sovereignty, but he does develop in us his love, joy, peaceableness, patience, kindness, goodness, faithfulness, gentleness and self-control, as they are perfectly exemplified in his dear Son.

What God has as perfection, we are to possess as a quality. He is glorified as our lives reflect his character. The words of our Lord Jesus emphasize this truth: 'This is to my Father's glory, that you bear much fruit, showing yourselves to be my disciples' (John 15:8). Our first aim in the desire for the growth of the Spirit's fruit is the glory of God. Such words can too quickly trip off our lips. God is not necessarily glorified by our saying that we are Christians, but he is when our lives and characters proclaim and confirm it. Our lives shine with his light as good deeds bring him praise (Matthew 5:16). As our Saviour glorified the Father by going about doing good (Acts 10:38), so we are to do the same.

The pre-eminence of the fruit of the Spirit

The fruit of the Spirit is more important than the gifts of the Spirit. In contrast to the first and pre-eminent aspect of the Spirit's fruit — love that never fails — prominent spiritual gifts like 'prophecies ... will cease ... tongues ... will be stilled ... knowledge ... will pass away' (1 Corinthians 13:8). While spiritual gifts have relevance only to this life, the fruit of the Spirit is of eternal duration.

When our Saviour returns, the development of the Spirit's fruit will be brought to its glorious completion as we are transformed into the likeness of the Lord Jesus (1 John 3:2). We will be like a mirror perfectly reflecting his glory. This will be there for all to see, and it will surpass all we could ever imagine. At the same time, we shall be so changed to be like him that he will be admired in us. When we look at a great work of art, we admire the artist. When the millions of the redeemed stand together, each of them his workmanship, changed into his likeness, the Lord Jesus will be admired, marvelled at and praised.

When we consider the fruit of the Spirit we may become discouraged or disheartened because we feel it is so little displayed in us. We should not be too dismayed. Those whose lives exhibit the best fruit seldom see it in themselves. The fruit is not something we readily recognize in ourselves. John Newton helpfully described his spiritual growth and sanctification: 'I am not what I ought to be, I am not what I want to be, I am not what I hope to be in another world, but still I am not what I once used to be, and by the grace of God I am what I am.'[3]

The book of Genesis describes a moving moment when Jacob told his sons what would happen to them in the years to come (Genesis 49:1). After many years of sadness and difficulty, Joseph had been restored to his father and brothers, and good had come to his whole family as well as to the Jewish people. Jacob's description of Joseph was apt and moving (although the picture of an apple tree may be more familiar and meaningful to us than a vine):

Joseph is a fruitful vine,
    a fruitful vine near a spring,
    whose branches climb over a wall

(Genesis 49:22).

Jacob's statement implies three conclusions.

1. Joseph's secret was declared: *he knew the source of his strength* — his roots went to a spring. Like the psalmist he could have said, 'All my fountains [or springs] are in you' (Psalm 87:7). His roots were in God, as our roots may be, through our spiritual union with the Lord Jesus Christ. The testimony of the book of Genesis is that 'the LORD was with him' (39:2, 21).

2. *Joseph's fruitfulness benefited those close to him, and others too.* His branches climbed over a wall. He brought help and refreshment to other people's lives, although he may have been unaware of it.

3. *Joseph's fruitfulness came only after the hard discipline of chastisement or pruning.* Joseph would not have been as fruitful as he was had he not passed through his difficult and bitter experiences. His character was pruned by his troubles. Nothing had been wasted.

Noteworthy conclusions

There are four conclusions from our consideration of the picture of fruit from which we can draw help.

1. *God's concern with our characters is greater than we may realize.* Busyness in Christian service is no substitute for character development. The people we are is more important than the work we do. Unconsciously, we may prefer to concentrate upon activity because it brings us into the limelight and fosters our pride. God sometimes removes us from a sphere of activity in order that concentration may be upon the development of our

character. We may live as much, if not more, for God's pleasure by our characters than by our Christian service and activity. (Moses' removal from his self-motivated activity in Egypt to years of shepherding a flock in Midian plainly had his character improvement in view.)

2. *There is a Christian character.* We speak of the Scottish, English, Welsh, Irish, French, German or American character, and so forth. By so doing, we imply that distinctive features exist that cannot be missed in the lives of those who belong to different areas of the world. Likewise, distinctive features cannot be missed in the lives of those who show that they belong to our Lord Jesus Christ. 'Therefore,' the New Testament concludes, 'if anyone is in Christ, he is a new creation; the old has gone, the new has come!' (2 Corinthians 5:17). The beauty and attractiveness of this Christian character is especially seen when we place it alongside the acts of the sinful nature, described in Galatians (5:19-21). These sinful acts tend to get worse as the years pass, whereas the fruit of the Spirit gets better as it grows.

3. *God alone can achieve this fruit in our lives.* Our effort and active involvement are required (2 Peter 1:5-9) but in dependence upon God the Holy Spirit who lives in us and is at work in us. It is 'the fruit *of the Spirit*'. The fruit is his unique product. An important truth to take into our understanding is that the Bible does not refer to the 'fruits' of the Spirit but 'the fruit'; that is to say, fruit in the singular. The idea is not that believers exhibit different aspects of the Spirit's fruit in their lives, but rather that the nine aspects of the Spirit's fruit so go together that they are to be displayed in every Christian. By nature, some of us are more patient and gentle than others, whereas they may be more faithful and self-controlled. God's grace makes *all* the fruit grow in us, as a complete whole. The different

features of the Spirit's fruit are like flowers growing together on the one stem. It is helpful to correct ourselves when we speak of the 'fruits' of the Spirit rather than the 'fruit'.

4. *God's purpose is that the Lord Jesus should have the pre-eminence* (Colossians 1:18). Nothing pleases the Father more than to see his Son's character reproduced in us. The Father's greatest pleasure and satisfaction is found in his Son. In the Old Testament he declared that satisfaction and delight in his description of the Messiah (Isaiah 42:1; cf. Matthew 12:18), and in the New Testament in his unique approval of his Son at both his baptism and transfiguration: 'This is my Son, whom I love; with him I am well pleased' (Matthew 3:17; Mark 9:7). It follows therefore that nothing gives the Father greater pleasure than to see his Son's character reproduced and reflected in us, 'the garden of his delight'. Christian holiness is our being made like him. As the Holy Spirit does this remarkable work in us, the Lord Jesus is honoured, since his saving work is the ground of it, and our conformity to his likeness its glory.

A vital test

The absence or presence of the Spirit's fruit will be the final assessment of our lives. The ultimate test will be applied on the Day of Judgement. The fruit of the Spirit has an eschatological element, therefore, in that it has relevance to what will happen at the return of our Lord Jesus Christ, when he will judge all, the living and the dead. In a different context, the Lord Jesus said, 'Every good tree bears good fruit, but a bad tree bears bad fruit. A good tree cannot bear bad fruit, and a bad tree cannot bear good fruit. Every tree that does not bear good fruit is cut down and thrown into the fire. Thus, by their fruit you will recognize them' (Matthew 7:17-20).

While, as the sower of the parable indicates, there are different levels of fruitfulness, God's assessment of our fruit will be perfect. What ultimately counts is not what others say of us, but what he says: 'For it is not the one who commends himself who is approved, but the one whom the Lord commends' (2 Corinthians 10:18). His commendation awaits those who live their lives now for his pleasure. Rather than waiting to see what the Day of Judgement reveals, we should test our lives now to avoid disappointment then (2 Corinthians 13:5).

References

1. Prologue

1. H. E. Hopkins, *Charles Simeon of Cambridge*, Hodder and Stoughton, p.46.

2. Love

1. George Orwell, *Down and Out in Paris*, Penguin Books, p.14.
2. Brian Mawhinney, *In the Firing* Line, HarperCollins, p.167.
3. Frederick M. Lehman, 'History of the Song', *The love of God*, 1948.
4. Stephen Neill, *A History of Missions*, Penguin Books, p.42.
5. *Longer Version, Chapter VI*, quoted in John Stott, *The Epistles of John*, InterVarsity Press, p.49.
6. G. F. Barbour, *Life of Alexander Whyte*, p.615.
7. Hopkins, *Charles Simeon of Cambridge*, p.166.
8. Iain Murray, *Diary of Kenneth MacRae*, Banner of Truth, p.33.
9. Hugh Anderson, *The Life and Letters of Christopher Anderson*, p.285.

3. Joy

1. Letter XXI, of *Rutherford's Letters*.

2. John Calvin, *The Institutes of Christian religion*, I, v, 8; I, vi, 2;
   and I, xiv, 20.
3. E. Peterson, *Answering God*, Marshall Pickering, p.72.
4. Iain Murray, *Jonathan Edwards*, Banner of Truth, p.36f.
5. *Ibid.*, p.36f.
6. Faith Cook, *William Grimshaw of Haworth*, Banner of Truth, p.278.
7. Murray, *Jonathan Edwards*, p.36f.
8. Quoted from *Adomnan's Life of Columba* by Stephen Neill in *A
   History of Christian Missions*, Penguin Books, p.69.
9. C. S. Lewis, *Letters to Malcolm*, Fount, p.90.
10. *The Guardian*, Thursday 12 October 1967.

4. Peace

1. Iain H. Murray, *David Martyn Lloyd-Jones: The First Forty Years*,
   Banner of Truth, p.239.
2. Faith Cook, *Samuel Rutherford and his friends*, Banner of Truth,
   p.126.
3. Nelson Mandela, *Long Walk to Freedom*, Little Brown & Co.,
   p.604.

5. Patience

1. William Dalrymple, *A Year in Delhi*, HarperCollins, p.62.
2. Quoted in Ian Barclay, *Down with Heaven*, Falcon Books, p.50.
3. Margaret Drewery, *William Carey*, Hodder and Stoughton, p.153ff.
4. J. C. Pollock, *Hudson Taylor and Maria*, Hodder and Stoughton,
   p.35.
5. Hugh Anderson, *The Life and Letters of Christopher Anderson*,
   p.297.

6. Kindness

1. Andrew Bonar, *Heavenly Springs*, Banner of Truth, p.10.

2. Frederick William Faber (1814-63), *Faber's Hymns*, p.43.
3. Charles Swindoll, *The Grace Awakening*, Word Publishing, p.222.
4. Martin H. Fischer, *Bloomsbury Treasury of Quotations*, Bloomsbury, p.375.
5. *Confessions 5: xiii.*

7. Goodness

1. E. J. Poole-Connor, *Evangelical Unity*, Fellowship of Independent Evangelical Churches, 1941, p.121.
2. Alfred Denning, *The Family Story*, Butterworth, p.19.

8. Faithfulness

1. G. C. Cragg, *Grimshaw of Haworth*, Canterbury Press, p.61.
2. C. H. Spurgeon, *The Early Years*, Banner of Truth, p.105.
3. Leslie Lyall, *Come Wind, Come Weather*, Hodder and Stoughton, pp.52, 58.
4. *The Scotsman*, 2 May 2001.
5. J. B. Phillips, *The Price of Success*, Hodder and Stoughton, p.75.
6. John Pollock, *Gordon - the man behind the legend*, Constable & Co. Ltd, pp.180, 216f.
7. Murray, *Diary of Kenneth MacRae*, p.460.
8. Eileen Crossman, *Mountain Rain*, OMF Books, p.13.
9. *Ibid.*, p.14.
10. Thomas Charles, *Spiritual Counsel,* Banner of Truth, p.384.

9. Gentleness

1. Mary Batchelor, *Catherine Bramwell Booth*, Lion Publishing, p.137.
2. Sheila Cassidy, *Sharing the Darkness*, Darton, Longman & Todd, p.94.

3. Jonathan Edwards, *The History of Redemption*, Religious Tract Society (1831), p.224.
4. Thomas Browne, *Christian Morals, III*, c. 1680.
5. John Cole, *As it seemed to me*, Weidenfeld and Nicholson, p.2.
6. Samuel Taylor Coleridge, in a satirical poem, published in 1799, entitled *The Devil's Thoughts*.
7. James Macnair, *Livingstone the Liberator*, Collins (1940).
8. Robert Mackenzie, *John Brown of Haddington*, Banner of Truth, p.30.
9. Arnold A. Dallimore, *George Whitefield*, Banner of Truth, I, p. 140; II, p.124.
10. Charles Smyth, *Cyril Forster Garbett, Archbishop of York*, Hodder and Stoughton, p.19.

10.   Self-control

1. Benjamin Franklin, *Life of Franklin*, Harper and Brothers (1848), p.24.
2. *Ibid.*, p.131.
3. R. Coad, *Laing: The Biography*, Hodder and Stoughton, p.48.
4. Peterson, *Answering God*, p.61.
5. John Pollock, *John Wesley*, Hodder and Stoughton, p.245.
6. *Chrysostom and his Message*, from the 33rd homily on Matthew. Trans. by S. Neill, London, 1962.
7. Andrew Bonar, *Diary and Letters*, Banner of Truth, p.279.
8. *Ibid.*, p.301.
9. Dorothy Clarke Wilson, *Ten Fingers for God*, Hodder and Stoughton, p.35f.
10. Roy Plomley, *Desert Island Discs*, Fontana, p.161.

11.   Postscript

1. Hopkins, *Charles Simeon of Cambridge*, p.101f.
2. Captain Cook's Journals, Tuesday, 24th August 1773.
3. John Stott, *The Contemporary Christian*, IVF, p.386.

Questions for further thought or discussion

1. Prologue
Read Galatians 5:16-26

1. Why does Paul use the word 'fruit' to describe Christian character?
2. Why the 'fruit' of the Spirit rather than the 'fruits'?
3. *Being* or *doing*? In which direction does the fruit of the Spirit point us?

2. Love
Read 1 Corinthians 13

1. Why does love come first in the list of the fruit of the Spirit?
2. How is God's love different from ordinary human love?
3. How has the Holy Spirit helped you to love someone you did not love before your new birth and conversion? Are there examples, probably best anonymously, that you can share?

3. Joy
Read Philippians 4:1-7

1. What makes joy different from happiness?

2. What is at the heart of a believer's joy? (See, for example, Romans 5:11 and 1 Peter 1:8-9.)
3. Where is the proper focus of our joy and how can we help ourselves to keep it right?

4. Peace

Read 1 Thessalonians 5:12-24

1. In what ways may it be costly to aim at peaceableness?
2. Which part of the human body contributes most to peaceableness or the lack of it?
3. Why is peaceableness so obviously part of true wisdom? (See, for example, James 3:13-18.)

5. Patience

Read 1 Peter 2:13-25

1. In what ways is God's patience described? (For example, in Exodus 34:6 and 1 Peter 3:20.)
2. Patience has three important aspects: patience with God, patience in waiting and patience in trials. Which was required of Abraham, Job and Timothy? See Genesis 22:17-18; James 5:10-11; 2 Timothy 2:24.
3. How is the Lord Jesus an example of patience in these three areas?

6. Kindness

Read Matthew 11:28-30

1. What do the Lord Jesus' words in Matthew 11:28-30 teach us about his kindness? Should these aspects of kindness be reproduced in us?

2. Luke 6:27-36 includes a reference to God the Father being 'kind to the ungrateful and wicked' (v. 35). In what ways in this passage does the Lord Jesus suggest that we should show similar kindness?
3. Why is kindness an important part of Christian witness?

7. Goodness
Read Ephesians 2:1-10

1. An illustration of goodness in Barnabas was the encouragement he gave to others (Acts 4:36). How important is the ministry of encouragement? Who needs it? Who ought to be exercising it and how?
2. While good works have no place in the obtaining of salvation, why are they a principal evidence of our experience of it? (See Matthew 5:16; Ephesians 2:10 and James 2:17.)
3. Did the good works and character of a Christian have any place in your conversion? If so, how?

8. Faithfulness
Read 1 Corinthians 10:1-13

1. Why is God's faithfulness important to us?
2. From what did the Lord Jesus Christ's faithfulness to his disciples flow? (See John 13:1 as one example.)
3. In what areas of life and relationships is faithfulness a priority?

9. Gentleness
Read Isaiah 42:1-4

Isaiah 42:1-4 is one of the Servant Songs that describes the character of our Lord Jesus Christ.

1. What aspects of his gentleness and meekness does it highlight?
2. Are gentleness and meekness commonly appreciated? Are they admired qualities?
3. In which situations in life is gentleness especially necessary? (If you have time, you may like to look up 2 Corinthians 10:1; 1 Thessalonians 2:7; 1 Timothy 3:3; Galatians 6:1.)

10. Self-control
Read Titus 2:1-15

1. In what ways do all or most aspects of the Spirit's fruit require the exercise of self-control?
2. Which 'acts of the sinful flesh' (Galatians 5:19-21) show an absence of self-control?
3. How important is the care of the mind in the achievement of self-control?

11. Postscript
Read Psalm 92 and 2 Peter 1:5-9

1. Why may the best fruit in our lives be towards its end?
2. What special fruit have you observed in believers who are much older than yourself?
3. How does the fruit of the Spirit in our lives contribute to the spiritual well-being of the whole body of Christ?
4. Why is the fruit of the Spirit more important than the gifts of the Spirit?
5. Which Bible characters stand out for their spiritual fruitfulness? Are you able to discern probable reasons for their fruitfulness?

Scripture index